Stephen:

Another world is possible.

John

D1067538

Social Movements, Civil Society, and Radical Adult Education

Critical Studies in Education and Culture Series

Becoming and Unbecoming White: Owning and Disowning a Racial Identity
Christine Clark and James O'Donnell

Critical Pedagogy: An Introduction, 2nd Edition
Barry Kanpol

Michel Foucault: Materialism and Education
Mark Olssen

Revolutionary Social Transformation: Democratic Hopes, Political Possibilities, and Critical Education
Paula Allman

Critical Reflection and the Foreign Language Classroom
Terry A. Osborn

Community in Motion: Theatre for Development in Africa
L. Dale Byam

Nietzsche's Legacy for Education: Past and Present Values
Michael Peters, James Marshall, and Paul Smeyers, editors

Rituals, Ceremonies, and Cultural Meaning in Higher Education
Kathleen Manning

Political Relationship and Narrative Knowledge: A Critical Analysis of School Authoritarianism
Peter B. Armitage

Education, Literacy, and Humanization: Exploring the Work of Paulo Freire
Peter Roberts

Critical Education Against Global Capitalism: Karl Marx and Revolutionary Critical Education
Paula Allman

Theory and Resistance in Education: Towards a Pedagogy for the Opposition, Revised and Expanded Edition
Henry A. Giroux, editor

Social Movements, Civil Society, and Radical Adult Education

John D. Holst
Foreword by Peter McLaren

Critical Studies in Education and Culture Series
Edited by Henry A. Giroux

Bergin & Garvey
Westport, Connecticut • London

Library of Congress Cataloging-in-Publication Data

Holst, John D.
    Social movements, civil society, and radical adult education / John D. Holst; foreword
by Peter McLaren.
       p.   cm. — (Critical studies in education and culture series, ISSN 1064–8615)
    Includes bibliographical references and index.
    ISBN 0–89789–811–7 (alk. paper)
    1. Adult education—Social aspects. 2. Social movements. 3. Civil society. 4.
Marxian economics. I. Title. II. Series.
    LC5225.S64H65   2002
    306.43'2—dc21   2001037641

British Library Cataloguing in Publication Data is available.

Copyright © 2002 by John D. Holst

All rights reserved. No portion of this book may be
reproduced, by any process or technique, without the
express written consent of the publisher.

Library of Congress Catalog Card Number: 2001037641
ISBN: 0–89789–811–7
ISSN: 1064–8615

First published in 2002

Bergin & Garvey, 88 Post Road West, Westport, CT 06881
An imprint of Greenwood Publishing Group, Inc.
www.greenwood.com

Printed in the United States of America

The paper used in this book complies with the
Permanent Paper Standard issued by the National
Information Standards Organization (Z39.48–1984).

10 9 8 7 6 5 4 3 2 1

Copyright Acknowledgments

The author and publisher gratefully acknowledge permission for use of the following material:

Excerpts from *Gramsci: Pre-Prison Writings* by Antonio Gramsci, edited by Richard Bellamy and translated by Virginia Cox (New York: Cambridge University Press, 1994). Reprinted with the permission of Cambridge University Press.

Excerpts from *Civil Society and Political Theory* by Jean L. Cohen and Andrew Arato (Cambridge, MA: MIT Press, 1992). Used by permission.

Excerpts from *Social Movements: A Cognitive Approach* by Ron Eyerman and Andrew Jamison (University Park, PA: Pennsylvania State University Press, 1991).

Excerpts from *Democracy and Civil Society* by John Keane (London: Verso, 1988), pp. xiii, 14–15, 58, 59, 60, 61, 62. Used by permission.

Excerpts from *German Ideology* by Karl Marx and Frederick Engels (Moscow: Progress, 1976). Used by permission.

Excerpts from "On the Jewish Question" by Karl Marx, in *Collected Works, Vol. III* by Karl Marx and Frederick Engels (New York: International, 1975). Used by permission.

Excerpts from *The Crowd and the Public and Other Essays* by Robert E. Park, edited by H. Elsner, Jr., and translated by C. Elsner (Chicago: University of Chicago Press, 1972). © 1972 by the University of Chicago. All rights reserved. Used by permission.

Excerpts from *Selections from the Prison Notebooks* by Antonio Gramsci, edited and translated by Quintin Hoare and Geoffrey Nowell Smith (New York: International, 1971). Used by permission.

Excerpts from *Basic Writings on Politics and Philosophy* by Karl Marx and Frederick Engels, edited by Lewis S. Feuer (Garden City, NJ: Anchor Books, 1959). Used by permission.

An earlier version of Chapter 5 appeared as "The Affinities of Lenin and Gramsci: Implications for Radical Adult Education Theory and Practice" in *The International Journal of Lifelong Education, 18*(5), 407–421. Copyright 1999. Reproduced by permission of Taylor & Francis, Inc., http://www.routledge-ny.com.

To Malicha

Contents

Series Foreword

Educational reform has fallen upon hard times. The traditional assumption that schooling is fundamentally tied to the imperatives of citizenship designed to educate students to exercise civic leadership and public service has been eroded. The schools are now the key institution for producing professional, technically trained, credentialized workers for whom the demands of citizenship are subordinated to the vicissitudes of the marketplace and the commercial public sphere. Given the current corporate and right wing assault on public and higher education, coupled with the emergence of a moral and political climate that has shifted to a new Social Darwinism, the issues which framed the democratic meaning, purpose, and use to which education might aspire have been displaced by more vocational and narrowly ideological considerations.

The war waged against the possibilities of an education wedded to the precepts of a real democracy is not merely ideological. Against the backdrop of reduced funding for public schooling, the call for privatization, vouchers, cultural uniformity, and choice, there are the often ignored larger social realities of material power and oppression. On the national level, there has been a vast resurgence of racism. This is evident in the passing of anti-immigration laws such as Proposition 187 in California, the dismantling of the welfare state, the demonization of black youth that is taking place in the popular media, and the remarkable attention provided by the media to forms of race talk that argue for the intellectual inferiority of blacks or dismiss calls for racial justice as simply a holdover from the "morally bankrupt" legacy of the 1960s.

Poverty is on the rise among children in the United States, with 20 percent of all children under the age of eighteen living below the poverty line. Unemployment is growing at an alarming rate for poor youth of color, especially in the urban centers. While black youth are policed and disciplined in and out of the nation's schools, conservative and liberal educators define education through the ethically limp discourses of privatization, national standards, and global competitiveness.

Many writers in the critical education tradition have attempted to challenge the right wing fundamentalism behind educational and social reform in both the United States and abroad while simultaneously providing ethical signposts for a public discourse about education and democracy that is both prophetic and transformative. Eschewing traditional categories, a diverse number of critical theorists and educators have successfully exposed the political and ethical implications of the cynicism and despair that has become endemic to the discourse of schooling and civic life. In its place, such educators strive to provide a language of hope that inextricably links the struggle over schooling to understanding and transforming our present social and cultural dangers.

At the risk of overgeneralizing, both cultural studies theorists and critical educators have emphasized the importance of understanding theory as the grounded basis for "intervening into contexts and power . . . in order to enable people to act more strategically in ways that may change their context for the better."[1] Moreover, theorists in both fields have argued for the primacy of the political by calling for and struggling to produce critical public spaces, regardless of how fleeting they may be, in which "popular cultural resistance is explored as a form of political resistance."[2] Such writers have analyzed the challenges that teachers will have to face in redefining a new mission for education, one that is linked to honoring the experiences, concerns, and diverse histories and languages that give expression to the multiple narratives that engage and challenge the legacy of democracy.

Equally significant is the insight of recent critical educational work that connects the politics of difference with concrete strategies for addressing the crucial relationships between schooling and the economy, and citizenship and the politics of meaning in communities of multicultural, multiracial, and multilingual schools.

Critical Studies in Education and Culture attempts to address and demonstrate how scholars working in the fields of cultural studies and critical pedagogy might join together in a radical project and practice informed by theoretically rigorous discourses that affirm the critical but refuse the cynical, and establish hope as central to a critical pedagogical and political practice but eschew a romantic utopianism. Central to such a project is the issue of how pedagogy might provide cultural studies theorists and educators with an opportunity to engage pedagogical practices that are not only transdisciplinary, transgressive, and oppositional, but also connected to a wider project designed to further racial, economic, and political democracy.[3] By taking seriously the relations between culture and power, we further the possibilities of resistance, struggle, and change.

Critical Studies in Education and Culture is committed to publishing work that opens a narrative space that affirms the contextual and the specific while simultaneously recognizing the ways in which such spaces are shot through with issues of power. The series attempts to continue an important legacy of theoretical work in cultural studies in which related debates on pedagogy are understood and addressed within the larger context of social responsibility, civic courage, and the reconstruction of democratic public life. We must keep in mind Raymond Williams's insight that the "deepest impulse (informing cultural politics) is the desire to make learning part of the process of social change itself."[4] Education as a cultural pedagogical practice takes place across multiple sites, which include not only schools and universities but also the mass media, popular culture, and other public spheres, and signals how within diverse contexts, education makes us both subjects of and subject to relations of power.

This series challenges the current return to the primacy of market values and simultaneous retreat from politics so evident in the recent work of educational theorists, legislators, and policy analysts. Professional relegitimation in a troubled time seems to be the order of the day as an increasing number of academics both refuse to recognize public and higher education as critical public spheres and offer little or no resistance to the ongoing vocationalization of schooling, the continuing evisceration of the intellectual labor force, and the current assaults on the working poor, the elderly, and women and children.[5]

Emphasizing the centrality of politics, culture, and power, *Critical Studies in Education and Culture* will deal with pedagogical issues that contribute in imaginative and transformative ways to our understanding of how critical knowledge, democratic values, and social practices can provide a basis for teachers, students, and other cultural workers to redefine their role as engaged and public intellectuals. Each volume will attempt to rethink the relationship between language and experience, pedagogy and human agency, and ethics and social responsibility as part of a larger project for engaging and deepening the prospects of democratic schooling in a multiracial and multicultural society. *Critical Studies in Education and Culture* takes on the responsibility of witnessing and addressing the most pressing problems of public schooling and civic life, and engages culture as a crucial site and strategic force for productive social change.

Henry A. Giroux

NOTES

1. Lawrence Grossberg, "Toward a Genealogy of the State of Cultural Studies," in Cary Nelson and Dilip Parameshwar Gaonkar, eds., *Disciplinarity and Dissent in Cultural Studies* (New York: Routledge, 1996), 143.

2. David Bailey and Stuart Hall, "The Vertigo of Displacement," *Ten* 8 2:3 (1992), 19.

3. My notion of transdisciplinary comes from Mas'ud Zavarzadeh and Donald Morton, "Theory, Pedagogy, Politics: The Crisis of the "Subject" in the Humanities," in *Theory Pedagogy Politics: Texts for Change*, Mas'ud Zavarzadeh and Donald Morton, eds. (Urbana: University of Illinois Press, 1992), 10. At issue here is neither ignoring the boundaries of discipline-based knowledge nor simply fusing different disciplines, but creating theoretical paradigms, questions, and knowledge that cannot be taken up within the policed boundaries of the existing disciplines.

4. Raymond Williams, "Adult Education and Social Change," in *What I Came to Say* (London: Hutchinson-Radus, 1989), 158.

5. The term "professional legitimation" comes from a personal correspondence with Professor Jeff Williams of East Carolina University.

Foreword

> [S]ettling everything for all times is not our task. What we have to do at present is the ruthless critique of all that exists, ruthless both in the sense of not being afraid of the results it arrives at and in the sense of being just as little afraid of conflict with the powers that be. ... We do not say to the world: "Cease your struggles, they are foolish; we will give you the true slogan of the struggle." We merely show the world why it really struggles, and that consciousness is something it has to acquire, even if it does not want to.
>
> —Karl Marx (letter to Arnold Ruge, September 1843, as cited in Merrifield, 2000, p. 15)

Much has been said about the crisis of capitalism that marks our current historical conjuncture. Capitalism continues to proceed apace, spreading its spiked wings, and each day scavenging for prey, sinking its bony talons into the backs of its helpless victims. As frightening as this economic *Chupacabra* might be, it fails to invoke fear in the ruling class, which has suckled the creature for centuries, directing it to feed upon only the poor and the vulnerable. Today, its victims are the billion who are prowling the streets, scavenging for food, and living on less than a dollar a day and those three billion others who try to make ends meet on less than two dollars a day (more than half the population of the world).

Education scholars are finally beginning to take a long-overdue notice of this beast and connect its selective appetite to advanced capitalism's missing persons lists. Educational researchers are finally directing their attention to the living contradictions of capital: the masses of the walking dead that populate our social universe (George, 2000). At last, policy researchers and sociologists in the field of education are no longer permitting the contradictions of the commodity process to remain below the surface of public attention. They are addressing head-on the fundamental contradiction between social production and private appropriation (Banfield, 2000) and exploring in labyrinthine detail the multiscalar, multisited, and market-driven globalization process.

We have arrived at a time when the gauntlet is being thrown down before the neoliberal free-marketeers, captains of industry, and Washington cartels of global carpetbaggers whose transborder mergers, acquisitions, and megadeals are intent on gouging the working class wherever in the world they might be found—which is, precisely, everywhere. In the process, critical education scholars are condemning the trust companies and monopolies, conglomerates and holding companies, protective tariffs and price-fixing, and even the World Bank and International Monetary Fund (IMF) themselves. The educational community is finally learning about the fetid underbelly of capitalism. The picture is enough to turn one's stomach. Susan George (2000) describes today's "carrion capitalism," revealing how brokerage houses and hedge funds have set up vulture funds "whose only mission is to seek out wounded companies and those whose privatization is being forced by the World Bank–IMF tandem" (p. 7). We are alerted to the fact that sweatshops continue to flourish throughout the United States, forcing their employees to work nearly eighty hours a week without paying them overtime. When these sweatshops are accused of cheating their employees, they simply declare bankruptcy and reappear under a new name. There are more stories to tell, of course, and those stories will be told.

After alerting us to the dangers of neoliberal orthodoxy's Washington consensus, financial and trade liberalization, the privatization of state-owned companies, deregulation, a rigorous enforcement of property rights, the current proliferation of finance capital and speculative flows, structural adjustment programs, and the IMF's shock-therapy recovery policy initiatives, educationalists are finally exploring the ramifications for schooling in terms of the current internationalization of production and consumption under the tutelage of *burgerliche gesellschaft* and the politics of education. Educational criticism has encountered a historical juncture where it can no longer ignore the Wall Street–Treasury–IMF complex; the oligopolistic structure of the transnational corporations; cycles of speculative lending and default; turbo-capitalism, in which unregulated financial trading protects Wall Street speculators but punishes third-world peoples; crony capitalism, in which elites defraud foreign investors and then maximize short-term gain at the expense of long-term stability; and forced liberalization of financial markets (Tabb, 1999). There is growing recognition that all of these connect in some way or another to current education policy, practice, and pedagogy.

For starters, larger amounts of the gross domestic product that developing nations used to spend on public services such as education and health have been, with little public opposition, put in the marketplace for bids by multinational and transnational corporations. The model of comprehensive, egalitarian public education that my generation grew up with is currently on the chopping block. Neoliberal strategies of privatization are now engulfing the globe, seemingly with no end in sight. No immediate alternatives to the social universe of capital have appeared on the horizon. There appears to be no human life beyond the infinitely expanding social universe of capital. Even our dreams of escape appear to be imprinted by the logic of the commodity.

While we welcome the analysis of corporate-driven globalization, there is cause for some disappointment. After all, the overwhelming majority of solutions to the dilemma of capitalist schooling that we are offered by the educational left amount to little more than making capitalism more egalitarian, more equitable, more accountable to the poor and to minority populations, and more friendly overall. This is fine as far as it goes, but in my estimation it does not go far enough. It doesn't go far enough because it doesn't challenge the basic laws of motion of capital and existing social relations of production.

All that changes with the publication of this book.

In the pages that follow, the analysis presented by John Holst takes progressive education and its challenges and turns them upside down. In *Social Movements, Civil Society, and Radical Adult Education*, Holst makes a brilliant case for a reassessment of much of what goes on in the field of adult education from the perspective of a dialectical and materialist conception of history. His analysis is within the tradition of Marxism-Leninism, a tradition much derided since the fall of the Soviet Union and the Eastern Bloc countries but one that—in some social science circles at least—is making a bold reappearance and gaining a new and appreciative readership along the way (Cole, Hill, McLaren, & Rikowski, 2000). One has only to witness the important appearance of Paula Allman's *Revolutionary Social Transformation* to gain some sense of the urgency— and scholarly sophistication—that classical Marxists are tabling in the discussion of schooling in general, and nonformal or adult education in particular. Holst's work joins with such efforts in a way that not only is important for understanding the role and future direction of adult education but also is indispensable for approaching the debates over educational reform and transformation that are occurring worldwide. It is a book of rare courage and formidable insight.

To fully appreciate the importance of the analysis offered in this book, it is worthwhile to summarize what it shares in common with classical Marxist analysis. What classical Marxists share in common is their commitment to understanding labor's value form, not only its faulty circuits and irregularities of circulation, problems of unequal distribution or patterns of consumption, its deficiencies related to technology, or its precarious metaphysical moorings. Maintaining that capital grounds all social mediation as a form of value, they argue that the substance of labor itself must be questioned, because doing so brings us closer to understanding the nature of capital's social universe, out of which our subjectivities are created. Karl Marx's value theory of labor does not attempt to reduce labor to an economic category alone but is illustrative of how labor as value form constitutes our very social universe, one that has been underwritten by the logic of capital. Value is not some hollow formality, neutral precinct, or barren hinterland emptied of power and politics but, as Glenn Rikowski (2000) of England notes, is the very matter and antimatter of Marx's social universe. The production of value is not the same as the production of wealth. The production of value is historically specific and emerges whenever labor assumes its dual character. This is most clearly explicated in Marx's discussion of the contradictory nature of the commodity form and the expansive capacity of the commodity known as labor power. For Marx, the commodity is highly unstable and nonidentical. Its concrete particularity (use value) is subsumed by its existence as value-in-motion or by what we have come to know as "capital" (value is always in motion because of the increase in capital's productivity that is required to maintain expansion). The issue here is not simply that workers are exploited for their surplus value but that all forms of human sociability are constituted by the logic of capitalist work.

Rikowski has written a lucid analysis of the implications of globalization for education that both deepens and extends much of the Marxist analysis of education that has focused primarily on state restructuring, the recomposition of work, requirements of industry and commerce, wage labor, the state, social class, equality, knowledge, and alienation. Rikowski writes from the perspective of the labor process itself. His premise is provocative yet compelling and perhaps deceptively simple: education is involved in the direct production of the one commodity that generates the entire social universe of capital in all of its dynamic and multiform existence—labor power. Within the social universe of capital, individuals sell their capacity to labor, their labor power, for a wage. Because we are included in this social universe on a differential and unequal basis, people can get paid above or below the value of their labor power. Because labor power is implicated in human will or agency, and because it is impossible for capital to exist without it, education can be redesigned within a social justice agenda that will reclaim labor power for socialist alternatives to human capital formation. Following Marx, Rikowski starts from the idea that the commodity (the economic "cell form," or DNA, of capitalist society) incorporates the basic structuring elements of capitalist society: value, use value, and exchange value posited on the basis of abstract labor as measured by labor time. As the products of capitalist production, commodities are divided by Marx into material commodities as well as labor power, the latter of which refers to the potential to labor. Labor power exists at the level of the market in a virtual form. This virtual existence is transformed into real social existence in the labor process itself, as commodities take the concrete form of use values. Use value has value only because abstract labor (as socially average labor power) is materialized in it. Labor power, then, is an aggregate of mental, physical, and personality traits that are exercised by individuals whenever they produce use values. It is a special type of commodity that generates the "substance" of capital, which is "value." Value is the social substance of capital in that it generates useful products that incorporate value. Education largely traffics in labor power; more precisely, it is intimately involved in the social production of labor power. Labor power in this sense is a living commodity that has the capacity to generate more value (surplus value) than is required to maintain its social existence as labor power. Socially average human labor power is the foundation of the abstract labor that forms value (abstract labor in this case rests upon the socially necessary labor time required to produce any use value under conditions normal for a given society). Socially average labor power constitutes not concrete labor but value. Education, therefore, is implicated in producing labor power, that very special commodity that generates three important products: value, surplus value (the lifeblood or social energy of capital), and capital itself. Labor power (or human capital, as it is known in capitalist society) includes cognitive skills, intellectual capacity, work attitudes, and personality traits that form the "seeds" by which society becomes capitalized. What capitalist enterprises bent on privatizing education desire above all else is high-quality labor power. This goal can be achieved by means of programmatically updating the labor power of students as part of international competition for the most productive and efficient knowledge economies. This is not only about wealth creation but also about social cohesion. Capital tries hard to displace class composition—to keep people adapting to frequent job changes—in order to defuse the potential power of the working class. A major point underscored by Rikowski is that capital's social drives are infinite and that results don't matter.

All of what I have said above pivots on a central qualification: that the abolition of capital simultaneously requires a transformation in the form of value as well as in the value form of labor. Only by directing our attention to the transformation of alienated labor to freely associated labor can we avoid the bureaucracy and despotism of failed socialist regimes. That is, only by developing a positive alternative to capital can we proceed apace on the road to emancipation. Building this alternative is what John Holst's book attempts to accomplish.

Holst sets out to differentiate the work of classical Marxist critique—as advocated by socialist adult educational scholars—from that produced by radical pluralists, neo-Marxists, and post-Marxists. Holst is able to map out a relative correspondence among positions that progressive adult educators take, and their implicit and explicit views of civil society, of the state, of class fractions and class struggle, of the character and role of social movements, and of the ongoing role that capitalism plays in the lives of educators and their students. Implicated in the views of these groups is the way that they conscript figures such as Marx, Antonio Gramsci, and Paulo Freire into the service of their various educational projects. Not only do these figures confer a special legitimacy to their positions, but they are used selectively; that is, they rely on certain misunderstanding of their work, a move that Holst finds problematic. Holst returns to the actual writings of Freire, Gramsci, and Marx to reveal the ways in which he believes that the radical pluralists, neo-Marxists, and post-Marxists have vulgarized and domesticated their work. He contrasts their interpretations of Freire, Gramsci, and Marx with those adult education scholars who work from a socialist, or Marxist, perspective.

Holst considers the terrain of the politics of social movements and civil society and maps it out in ways that are profoundly illuminating, so much so that his treatise will be cause for much-needed debate on the radical left. With this book, Holst joins the leading figures in adult and nonformal education—Paula Allman, John Wallis, Frank Youngman, Peter Mayo, and others—in provoking a radical reconceptualization of revolutionary politics and what it means in the current historical conjuncture. For instance, Holst is not convinced that we have entered a postindustrial economy in which production can be moved easily from advanced capitalist countries in the North (the northern hemisphere) to developing countries in the South (the southern hemisphere). As Kim Moody (1997), whom Holst cites, has noted, most production still occurs in the North and most foreign direct investment is still controlled by the North. In fact, 80 percent of this investment is invested in the North itself. While it is true that northern industries are being transplanted to the South to take advantage of the cheaper labor markets, the North merely modernizes its economic base by making it more technologically sophisticated. Holst also doesn't believe that the state has dramatically withered away under the Silicon Valley onslaught of an information economy or the derealized character of information-based capital. In fact, he argues along with other socialist adult educators that, if anything, we have witnessed not the diminution of state power but its dramatic augmentation. This does not mean, however, as many radical pluralist and civil societarians argue, that we have experienced a qualitative rupture in capitalist relations of production since World War II. By contrast, revolutionary socialists such as Holst argue that we still live within monopoly capitalism or late capitalism. Internationally, the struggle between capital and labor as part of the practice of imperialism has not recorded any seismic shift that warrants world-historical reconsideration. The world still lives under the iron fist of imperialist social relations, only today that fist wears a velvet glove with a Nike swoosh on the thumb. Consequently, the privileged agent for fundamental social change must remain the working class, with the state still serving as the central target of its revolutionary struggle. This is because the state is still the main agent of globalization; it continues to maintain the conditions of accumulation, undertakes a rigid disciplining of the labor force, flexibly enhances the mobility of capital while ruthlessly suppressing the mobility of labor, and serves as a vehicle for viciously repressing social movements through such state apparatuses as the police, the military, and the judicial system. Take the example of the United States. Under the cover of globalization, the United States is taking the dangerous foreign policy initiative of unilateralism or exceptionalism and claiming that, as the world's most superior democracy, the United States should be exempt from world norms and that agreements such as the 1972 Anti-Ballistic Missile Treaty, the Kyoto treaty on global warming, and the Comprehensive Test Ban Treaty should be disregarded because they are no longer in the interests of the United States. Disregarding the advice of other nations is now a much greater likelihood with the current Bush administration, as the United States straps on its guns to assume the global role of the Lone Ranger.

That the state is still the major target of working-class struggle should be clearly evident, Holst argues, in the recent mass political strikes in France, South Korea, Italy, Belgium, Canada, Panama, South Africa, Brazil, Argentina, Paraguay, Bolivia, Greece, Spain, Venezuela, Haiti, Columbia, Ecuador, Britain, Germany, Taiwan, Indonesia, Nigeria, and elsewhere.

Holst remains skeptical of the new social movements dedicated to democratizing civil society but leaving the state apparatuses largely untouched. He is not interested in ways to democratize civil society if that means (and it usually does) that capitalism will be strengthened in the process. Proponents of the new social movements mistakenly believe that industrial production has declined in relevance; they engage in a self-limiting radicalization of the public sphere, largely struggle on behalf of bourgeois rights for the petite-bourgeoisie, fail to consider the state as a unitary agent of intervention and action in promoting structural reform, and eschew the goal of revolutionary Marxists of taking over the state and the economy. In fact, Holst notes that at a time when segments of the left have embraced a politics of discursive struggle and fragmentation, capitalism as a world economic system has become more universal and unified.

Central to Holst's analysis is the way in which progressive adult educators rely mightily on the concept of civil society. Unlike socialists, radical pluralists and civil societarians wish to portray civil society as largely free from the tentacles of the state. In order to contest such a view, Holst reads their work directly against the writings of Georg Hegel, Marx, and Gramsci.

Hegel essentially saw civil society as a realm of the particular where the alienated idea culminates in the realization of the idea in the state. For Hegel the state becomes the site where the alienation experienced in civil society is overcome, but Marx criticized Hegel's notion of civil society and the state as an imaginary idealist relation. For Marx, the state was another form of alienation, a central site of ruling-class oppression. Marx believed that the bourgeois revolutions of the eighteenth century abolished the political character of civil society so that "unpolitical man" appears as the "natural man." However, while the bourgeois state embodies "political man," it is not, in Marx's view, the place where human liberation is won. By contrast, it is a site where individuals are "endowed with an unreal universality." The state becomes a means for civil society to create the natural cosmopolitan citizen.

One of Holst's major premises is that where adult educators locate themselves on the radical pluralism–socialist divide largely determines their position on the question of political alliances. Rejecting Vladimir Lenin's dream of taking over the state and Marx's dream of overthrowing the rule of capital as outmoded, irrelevant, and romantic, the radical pluralists, according to Holst, largely champion the causes of the new progressive social movements and organizations dealing with feminism, antiracism, sexuality, and environmental issues because they view these as a necessary defense of the lifeworld and a courageous deepening of democracy through their engagements with civil society. While some socialist adult educationalists seek to forge alliances between the old (community-labor organizations and trade unions) and new social movements, others reject the new social movements outright. For the most part, they reject the new social movements on the basis that they depart from the basic tenets of classical Marxism, especially when read directly against the work of Marx and Gramsci. Many socialist adult educators, such as Allman and Wallis, believe that while the issues addressed by the new social movements are urgent and important, they nevertheless constitute what Gramsci would call "secondary questions." Consequently, they believe that forging a counter-hegemonic bloc with new social movements could be problematic, and it should be encouraged only when the primacy of working-class struggle against capital remains the overwhelming objective. Holst himself unapologetically takes such a position, arguing that what is important is not counter-hegemonic struggle but, as Lenin would advocate, the struggle for proletarian hegemony.

Radical pluralists generally embrace similar positions on the globalization of capital, civil society, and the role of the state. They generally remain faithful to the strong globalization thesis that makes the assumption that humanity has entered a qualitatively new epoch, breaking away from the industrial (Fordist) era of modernization and entering the new world of globalization, in which the economy is operating at a transnational level and where the nation-state is no longer the main political formation in control of the economy. Hence, the major actors can be found in the realm of civil society in the form of new social movements and nongovernmental organizations (NGOs) that work to expand, extend, defend, and strengthen civil society as well as to render it dramatically more ethnically inclusive. The radical pluralists and civil societarians view civil society as a natural progression after the defeat of feudalism. It is in the work of the radical pluralists and civil societarians that civil society takes on new importance through a more "activist" role, since it seemingly operates in a position that is relatively autonomous from the state and the market, thanks to the ongoing informal and non-formal efforts of the new social movements and their accompanying NGOs to advance the cause and the practice of citizenship. It is the arena of civil society where public policies of social justice can be pursued in a spirit of cooperation and civic participation and where a civil societarian adult education approach can be enacted within a reform-oriented politics of inclusion, influence, and democratic accountability. Here civil society is perceived as inherently benign, the primary site of dialogue and identity formation. Of course, as Holst notes, civil society is not antiseptically removed from the social relations of production, and it has even become staked out by neoliberals, many of whom take up residence within its comfortable precincts. Civil societarianism is perfectly compatible with the emphasis that free-marketeers place on self-sufficiency, enterprise zones, "capacity building," and grassroots empowerment initiatives. However, what is worse, in Holst's view, is that it simply transfers the costs of structural reform onto civil society. For instance, in arguing for personal and community responsibility in schemes like the self-management of public housing and public schools and the privatization of welfare, radical pluralists and civil societarians derail the guaranteeing of basic social services by the state.

In order to strengthen his case for socialism, and to rescue Gramsci from the grasp of the radical pluralists and civil societarians who have weakened and vulgarized the political center of gravity that informs

Gramsci's revolutionary theories, Holst turns to the work of socialist adult educators. Holst's reading of Gramsci dovetails with scholars such as Allman and Wallis who contend that Gramsci did not have in mind loose coalitions of social movements when he spoke of creating a historical bloc in civil society. To argue the contrary would be to distort in no small way his legacy as a committed communist and an advocate of Lenin. The war of position and the creation of proletarian hegemony requires class alliances that will allow the proletariat to mobilize the majority of the working population against capitalism and the bourgeois state. Holst argues that it is crucial to understand Gramsci within the historical context of his struggle to create proletarian hegemony and his view of the role of the working class as a revolutionary class, and this includes the important stress he places on the pedagogical dimensions of the revolutionary party. Thus, it is impossible to engage Gramsci through truncated "selected readings" that serve to isolate his ideas on civil society from the *leitmotif* of his work and the major trajectory of his political project, something we have seen over and over again in the work of the radical pluralists and civil societarians. Following Allman and Wallis, Holst resituates Gramsci—including his ideas of the state, the political party, organic intellectuals, spontaneity, hegemony, and alliances—within the corpus of Marx and Lenin's work. As a result we learn that Gramsci positioned civil society as a fundamental aspect of the state—more specifically, as a private, hegemonic apparatus of the state that was protected by "the armor of coercion." Even if one concedes that Gramsci saw private, civil society as distinct from the state, or political society, it is absolutely certain that he saw both as constituting part of the superstructure or the domain of ruling-class economic power and political interest. In other words, civil society is the site where the ruling class exerts its authority over the social order. Once the working class has seized state power, a postrevolutionary condition arises. During this period of the dictatorship of the proletariat, civil society can play a fundamental role in the creation of proletarian hegemony through the efforts of a vanguard of working-class organic intellectuals within the party— a party, it should be noted, that Gramsci likened to the role of a school. The key point that Holst makes here is that "Gramsci is not, like civil societarians, advocating the building or protecting of the existing bourgeois civil society, but the continuing creation of proletarian hegemony in a postrevolutionary situation." The idea of counter-hegemony speaks to a broad coalition of multiclass formations that in a larger sense undermines the very trajectory of the proletarian socialist movement. The struggle for a communist social formation must be first and foremost. Furthermore, Holst notes that Gramsci did not glorify the spontaneous rebelliousness of the working class but rather "consistently advocated for the necessity of the party to educate this spontaneity, to give it a consciousness of its historic potential."

Holst's analysis of the reach and role of hegemony is richly detailed and unambiguous. Individuals consent to the dominant ideology because of the position of the dominant group in the world of production. The dominant hegemony is shaped by the class that is the ruling material force in society. Hegemony is exerted not only in civil society but also at the point of production. The idea of counter-hegemony was never used by Gramsci because it speaks overwhelmingly to a reformist politics. Holst is an educator whose project is clearly directed not toward reformism but rather to transformation. He invokes John Ehrenberg in arguing that socialists have not suffered from an excess of orthodoxy but from insufficient fidelity to socialism's roots. In arguing so, Holst throws down the gauntlet before those who would consign socialism to the dustbin of history. He is in solidarity with Marx's concept of emancipation when he writes that "human emancipation is the overcoming of the alienation represented in the separation of political power (the state) and the social relations of production." A state is only necessary, notes Holst, "in a social formation based on exploitation." This brings us to the following question: Can a rejuvenated civil society populated by new ideas for democratizing the state overthrow the material conditions that enable capital to accumulate? Holst realizes that as a result of each and every solution—democratic or otherwise—offered by capital (through the reformist efforts of neo-Marxists, radical pluralists, and civil societarians) to the suffering of labor, labor will continue to suffer.

This is a book that should be read not only by students and professors of adult education but by educationalists who work in policy, curriculum, sociology of education, and the philosophy of education. It is also a book that will be welcome reading by educational activists. In this book I recognized positions that I formerly held and which I no longer advocate, such as a leftist, postmodernist, radical pluralist support of radical democracy. As a Marxist-Leninist I am aware of the controversy and passion—and in some cases perfunctory dismissal—that Holst's book will elicit. Yet I am confident that this book will help to deepen and extend the debate on the role that capitalism and democracy are playing on the stage of history.

Holst notes that socialism is not an incremental building upon or expansion of bourgeois democratic freedoms; it is about transferring power directly to the working class. This is a challenge that is not popular today, which makes it all the more essential that this book be read by everyone who cares about the future of human society.

Peter McLaren

REFERENCES

Banfield, G. (2000). Schooling and the spirit of enterprise: Producing the power to labor. *Education and Social Justice, 2* (3), 23–28.

Cole, M., Hill, D., McLaren, P., & Rikowski, G. (2000). *Red chalk: On schooling, capitalism, and politics*. London: Tufnell Press.

George, S. (2000, Winter). Another world is possible. *Dissent, 48* (1), 5–8.

Merrifield, A. (2000). Phantoms and spectres: Capital and labor at the millennium. *Environment and Planning D: Society and Space, 18*, 15–36.

Moody, K. (1997). *Workers in a lean world: Unions in the international economy*. London: Verso.

Rikowski, G. (2000, September). Messing with the explosive commodity: School improvement, educational research and labor-power in the era of global capitalism. In "If We Aren't Pursuing Improvement, What Are We Doing?" Symposium conducted at the Seventh British Educational Research Association Conference, Session 3.4, Cardiff University, Wales.

Tabb, W. K. (1999). Are new trade wars looming? *Monthly Review, 51* (6), 22–34.

Preface

This work represents the current status of my ongoing thinking about the relationship between education and social change. Along with my participation in various social movements, it was in the world of community-based adult education and community colleges that I began to consciously explore and formally study the relationship between education and social movements. This study is the outgrowth of this reflection and my past experience. It reflects a continuous unease I have felt in confronting the limits inherent in all social movement practice, and this, I think, the reader will find throughout the work. Although I have come to the commonly held understanding that we can and should struggle from whatever social location in which we find ourselves—one not necessarily better positioned than the other—we must do so from a carefully thought-out theoretical stance. I believe that it is vital for all adult educators to continuously engage radical theory in and out of the field. I hope this study can act as an introduction to a radical theory of social movements and civil society and as an invitation for further investigation into this important and often neglected area for adult educators.

In my own investigations into this area and its reflection in adult education, I have grown concerned with the abandonment of major tenets of the long tradition of Marxism. For more than 150 years, thousands have engaged in profound theoretical and practical struggles over the nature of capitalism and the possibilities of what Paula Allman (1999) calls "revolutionary social transformation." Beginning before, but accelerating with, the events of 1989, we have witnessed the rise of neo-Marxism and post-Marxism, leading to an outright abandonment of Marxism by many who made significant contributions to the tradition. At the moment of capitalist triumphalism in 1989–1990, its antithesis, Marxism, falters in what is partially a self-inflicted "crisis." At the moment when even bourgeois critics admit to the explanatory power of Marxism's analysis of the contemporary nature of capitalism, many of its longtime adherents seem won over by the antithetical temptations of postmodernism and the shortsightedness of mainstream clichés about the end of the nation-state. At the moment when those on the left were freed from the fetters of having to make excuses for "self-proclaimed" socialist states, they abandon the struggle for what they once argued could be "authentic forms of socialism." At the moment when we are witnessing capitalism overcoming the seventy-year delay in its full passage to the stage Lenin (1917/1939) labeled "imperialism" in the wake of the very revolution that caused this delay, many on the left have shunned this thinker and his analysis for a form of what I call "left-wing neoliberalism" in calls for building civil society through privatized development schemes.

A critique of these contradictions within radical adult education and the left in general is at the heart of this study. I am well aware of the immensity of the task at hand in rejuvenating a Marxist critique within adult education. I am also encouraged by recent studies (e.g., Allman, 1999; Brown 1999; Foley, 1999; McLaren, 2000; Murphy, 2000; Youngman, 2000) that also challenge radical adult educators to reassess our doubting and abandonment of the Marxist tradition in favor of postmodernism and radical pluralism. It is my hope that this study will be a part of a growing number of works that seek to reinject the Marxist tradition into radical adult education in our ongoing assessments as the dust settles in the post-1989 period. Reacquainting ourselves with this strand of our own tradition can go a long way in explaining the situation in which we currently find ourselves.

In the broader realm of educational studies, some scholars (Apple, 1996; Kincheloe, Steinberg, & McLaren, 1998) have insisted upon more unity between postmodernist and neo-Marxist perspectives to avoid what they see as self-destructive polemics that hinder the development of common ground. To a certain extent the current conjuncture of neoliberal triumph necessitates and leaves little room for anything other than practical alliances among Marxists and radical pluralists. Those of us, however, who see within the current conjuncture the possibilities of change qualitatively distinct from current practices must continue to advance our theory by maintaining the relevant elements of our long tradition, through political economic research of the present situation, and by drawing theoretical distinctions between ourselves and others in the field. The arguments I outline in this study are intended to do the latter.

There are several people at Northern Illinois University that I would like to thank for their contributions to this work. Phyllis Cunningham is a friend and model practitioner. She consistently created the intellectual space for me to explore the issues I deal with in this study. Meg George's knowledge and understanding of theory and history are benchmarks for my own development. Norm Stahl has been a mentor and friend, assisting me every step of the way. The members of the Capital and Class seminar (María Alicia Vetter, Mark Murphy, Carole Sassine, and Tarina Galloway) were fundamental in the conceptualization of this study. Kay Harned provided friendship, encouragement, and the opportunity for research work. The Graduate School of Northern Illinois University awarded me a generous fellowship for the 1999–2000 academic year that went a long way in providing financial assistance in the writing stage of this study.

At the University of St. Thomas, the School of Education and in particular Eleni Roulis and Christene Sirois provided me the time and necessary resources and assistance, respectively, for the preparation of the manuscript.

Numerous friends in academia and the social movements have provided inspiration, guidance, and encouragement. I would like to thank Henry Giroux for his kind consideration of my work. At Bergin & Garvey I would like to thank Jane Garry for her expert help and patience and Nicole Cournoyer and Judith Antonelli for their careful editing of the manuscript. Special thanks go to Peter McLaren, who so generously offered to write a Foreword to the text.

Finally, my family has supported me throughout the entire process.

Contextualizing the Contemporary Interest in Social Movements and Civil Society in Radical Adult Education Theory and Practice

A great deal of dramatic effect could be gained by beginning this work with a statement indicating that the field of adult education is at an important crossroad, a moment at which a decision must be made, or that it confronts a millennial opportunity to start afresh. Such a beginning would certainly help to justify the study, but it would also be based on false premises. Although today we *are* faced with a choice, it is the choice that Rosa Luxemburg (1916/1970b) laid out for us in the early part of the twentieth century: socialism or barbarism. Yet this choice was starkly apparent throughout the twentieth century. In the 1930s, for example, Paul Robeson (1958), faced with the growing threat of fascism, felt the urgency of this choice when speaking of his support of the Spanish Republic. "Every artist, every scientist, must decide *now* where he stands. He has no alternative. There is no standing above the conflict on Olympian heights. . . . The artist must elect to fight for Freedom or for Slavery. I have made my choice. I had no alternative" (p. 52). Later in the century, in the early 1960s, Mario Savio, a leader of the Berkeley Free Speech Movement, said the following in a speech:

There's a time when the operation of the machine becomes so odious, makes you so sick at heart, that you can't take part, you can't even tacitly take part. And you've got to put your bodies upon the gears and upon the wheels, upon the levers, upon all the apparatus and you've got to make it stop. And you've got to indicate to the people who run it, to the people who own it, that unless you're free, the machine will be prevented from working at all. (Cited in Bloom & Breines, 1995, pp. 111–112)

At the end of the century, Samir Amin confirmed the growing urgency of Luxemburg's choice. "More than ever humanity is confronted with two choices: to let itself be led by capitalism's unfolding logic to a fate of collective suicide or, on the contrary, to give birth to the enormous human possibilities carried by that world-haunting specter of communism" (cited in McLaren, 2000, p. 111). Heaney (1993) outlines the tension of the competing paradigms around this choice in the history of twentieth-century adult education. "Adult education has evolved in two paths. One has facilitated democratic reflection and action through a critical identification of issues; the other has served to domesticate learners, ignore contradictions, and adjust minds to the inevitable conformities of a mass society" (pp. 19–20).

In short, we always face this choice. Dialectics, however, teaches us that our world is in constant motion and change, and therefore we are forever put in the situation of having to reassess our choice based on the objective and subjective conditions of the moment. A dialectical and materialist concept of history teaches us that even though at any given point in history a particular mode of production (slavery, feudalism, capitalism, etc.) is predominant, due to the constant motion and change of society every mode of production has its time of reckoning, marking a period of social revolution or transformation in which we witness a qualitative change to a new mode of production. The task of radical adult education should be to make evident through dialogical investigation the relationship between the subjective and objective elements of this transformation. If we do not fall into economic determinism, we understand that we transform our society through our daily interactions with the natural and social world, yet rarely does this understanding grasp the interconnectedness of ourselves and others, institutions, nature, and social transformation. The task of political economy is to investigate the laws of motion of social transformation, thereby revealing opportunities of qualitative social transformation.

A political economic study would begin to address central questions of the day. First, was the twentieth century an epoch of qualitative social transformation from capitalism to socialism? Second, given the numerous self-proclaimed socialist revolutions of the twentieth century that have now almost without exception ended, has an epoch of qualitative social transformation come and gone? Third, can we still speak of the possibilities of qualitative social transformation today and in the future? The doubts raised by these questions have come to be called the *crisis of Marxism*.

This study enters the debate around these questions at a much higher level of abstraction (see Sweezy, 1942, Chapter 1, for an explanation of levels of abstraction), addressing the nature of this debate within the literature of radical adult education. This study is an effort toward a theoretical response to the latest version of "revisionism" in radical theory embodied in the advocation of new social movements as the qualitatively new agent of social change operating in the realm of civil society. To this end, it confines itself to a critical review of the literature in and outside radical adult education concerning the debates over social movements and the related theoretical concept of civil society that are playing an increasingly important role in the larger question of addressing the crisis of Marxism. This study is not intended to provide a political economic investigation of the current prospects of social revolution, but to critically analyze and provide an outline of the contemporary debates within radical adult education over the crisis of Marxism and the role assigned to social movements operating in civil society in overcoming this crisis.

What exactly is the nature of this crisis of Marxism? The current crisis of Marxism can be seen as one more crisis in a long history of crises since at least the defeats of the revolutions of 1848. Moreover, this current crisis at the end of the twentieth century has many parallels to the "'crisis of Marxism' which erupted at the turn of the [nineteenth] century" (Colletti, 1972, p. 59), codified in Eduard Bernstein's (1899/1911) *Evolutionary Socialism*. Both crises have at least three commonalities: (a) they are directly related to capitalism's continued ability to respond to and "overcome" economic crisis; (b) they share doubts over the continued possibility of revolution; and (c) they are characterized by a turn away from theory toward practice. Let's look at each of these points of comparison in turn.

First, the crisis of Marxism at the turn of the nineteenth century followed on the heels of recovery from "The Great Depression, which started in 1873 and . . . continued into the middle '90's" (Dobb, 1963, p. 300) and was characterized fundamentally by a crisis of overproduction that led capital to seek solutions through an imperialist search for markets that McCormick (1967) calls "exporting the social question." Similarly, the contemporary crisis of Marxism comes at a time when capital has, at least in the United States, seemingly resolved the long downturn of the 1970s and 1980s and is so triumphantly proclaiming its resilience, most obviously shown by the fall of actually existing socialism, that its apologists have declared an "end to history."

Second, at these points of capitalist "recovery," a fundamental question for the left emerges. "Is the time of social revolution past or not? Have we already the political conditions which can bring about a transition from capitalism to socialism without political revolution, without the conquest of political power by the proletariat, or must we still expect an epoch of decisive struggles for the possession of this power and therewith a revolutionary epoch?" (Karl Kautsky [1902], cited in Mills, 1962, p. 173). Kautsky raises the question in response to Eduard Bernstein's affirmative answer to this question of the end of an era of revolutionary possibilities. Today, lacking highly organized mass socialist or social democratic parties, the issue is hardly even raised as an interrogative.

What is now in crisis is a whole conception of socialism which rests upon the role of Revolution, with a capital 'r', as the founding moment in the transition from one type of society to another, and upon the illusory prospect of a perfectly unitary and homogeneous collective will that will render pointless the moment of politics. The plural and multifarious character of contemporary social struggles has finally dissolved the last foundation for that political imaginary.... Today, the left is witnessing the final act of the dissolution of that Jacobin imaginary. (Laclau & Mouffe, 1985, p. 2)

Third, the criticism that Rosa Luxemburg (1900/1970a) launched at revisionist practice one hundred years ago stands as well in today's crisis.

What appears to characterize this practice above all? A certain hostility to "theory." This is quite natural, for our "theory," that is, the principles of scientific socialism, impose clearly marked limitations to practical activity—insofar as it concerns the aims of this activity, the means used in attaining these aims, and the method employed in this activity. It is quite natural for people who run after immediate "practical" results to want to free themselves from such limitations and to render their practice independent of our "theory." (pp. 123–124)

Of contemporary radical adult education, Thompson (1980b) makes the following comment: "There are a number of reasons to explain why adult educators seem to underestimate the value of theory. Most of them are to do with the ramifications of being 'practical people' who judge credibility in terms of action.... In our discussions with adult educators, consequently, we have sensed a preference for descriptive rather than analytical accounts of practice" (p. 220). Twenty years later, Youngman (2000), specifically in reference to development but applicable to most areas of the field, says, "the writing in this field consists mainly of descriptive accounts of adult education activities, reports of program evaluations, and the results of small-scale empirical research projects. There have been few attempts to address the question of adult education and development at a theoretical level" (pp. 2–3).

As a direct result of, and playing a part in, this crisis of Marxism, the politics of social movements and civil society have become the dominant paradigm within radical adult education today. To begin, it is necessary to define some terminology. Though not explicitly defined in the literature, I use the term *radical adult education* to describe adult education theory and practice dedicated to significant social transformation within the left-wing political tradition. I say *significant* social transformation in order to include what have traditionally been called social democratic practices or reforms. Fundamental or qualitative transformation would exclude these more reformist practices for a concentration on revolutionary politics and adult education. I say *left wing* to purposefully exclude the politics of right-wing movements, which could also be labeled as radical in their goals but which are ultimately reactionary and conservative. Therefore, radical adult education speaks to those adult educators and theories that attempt to understand and promote the relationship between adult education and reformist or revolutionary social transformation. By the *politics of social movements,* I refer to the perceived potential of social movements to be effective agents of significant social transformation.

Radical adult education has a long history. This history, however, is not well documented, particularly in the United States in contrast to Great Britain, where the radical tradition of adult education has a more significant space in the literature. The marginalization of the radical tradition is due to several factors. First, as a recognized academically based field, it is relatively young, and therefore much work is still unfinished in the construction of its history. Second, precisely because adult education, which has occurred for as long as there have been adults, is now an increasingly professionalized field within a capitalist economic system, its significant radical tradition is being forced to the margins. In its place, human resource development (HRD) has emerged as the dominant paradigm for the field as a whole. Third, the majority of radical adult education before and during the time that adult education emerged as a field of study has occurred in settings not necessarily considered educational, and it has been practiced by people not necessarily considered by those in the field—or by themselves, for that matter—as educators. Specifically, much of the radical adult education that has taken place, largely informally, has occurred in meetings, protests, cultural events, and the day-to-day activities of social movements and organizations instigated by people who do not necessarily consciously consider the educational aspects of what they are doing. In addition, when these activists engage in explicitly educational activities—study groups, speaking and lecturing, leafleting, and so forth—they often label it party or movement work without separating it out as specifically adult education. In other words, the field of adult education and the activists overlook much vital educational work for politics; nevertheless, I would argue that within the radical political tradition, we can most likely find a parallel "field of adult education" with its own pedagogical tradition yet to be discovered by those of us who call ourselves adult educators.

Within the field itself, however, radical adult education has carved out a space for itself, and this study is an effort to enter the current debate within this tradition over the continued possibility of radical social change, the organizational forms this change can and should take, and the nature of adult education for social change within these organizational forms. As already stated, this debate is shaped by the wider context of the crisis of Marxism. Within radical adult education, as in radical politics generally, there is a dominant position that argues for a need to revise our political thinking in light of the changing political economic context. Traditionally, radical adult educators looked to what are now called *old social movements*, mainly working-class political parties and trade unions, as the principal organizational forms for social change. Several factors in the post–World War II period have led radical adult educators to reassess their privileging of these working-class organizational forms.

First, in the capitalist first world, these old social movements became increasingly integrated into the welfare state regimes. It is often argued that these old social movements formally, and at times informally, traded greater material benefits in the form of higher wages and institutionalized benefits, such as unemployment insurance and health care, for higher productivity and peaceful forms of protest. Second, many radical adult educators understood that the old social movements in the socialist states were absorbed by centralized party apparatuses to a point of losing their ability for independent action. Radical adult educators generally considered these regimes to be authoritarian and antithetical to "authentic" socialism. Third, in the capitalist third world, old social movements were largely destroyed by imperialist-backed right-wing military governments. Fourth, beginning mainly in the 1960s, organizational forms with seemingly a new type of politics (uninterested in the state or economy) and a new constituency (a new middle class in the capitalist first world and outside the working-class organizations in the capitalist third world and the socialist states) emerged as the fundamental agents of social change. With the fall of most socialist states and the related emergence of a dominant neoliberal economic model, the privileging of these new social movements accelerated. For many radical adult educators, the failure of self-proclaimed socialist states, which they believed oppressed workers rather than liberated them, along with the dissolution of many working-class parties in other parts of the world, marked the end of working-class political parties as viable agents of social change. In addition, globalization (loosely defined in the literature, as we shall see in Chapter 2), with its seemingly free-flowing capital and accompanying feebled nation-state, has made it virtually impossible for working-class trade unions to use solidarity from below or state intervention from above to protect the ever more fragile gains they made in the post–World War II period.

The new social movements (feminist, environmentalist, peace, identity, and autonomy movements) have replaced old social movements as the preferred organizational forms of social change for the majority of radical adult educators. From a British perspective, Yarnit (1980) captures the early enthusiasm of radical adult educators for these new movements.

We are living ... through the most promising revival of independent ... adult education since ... the 1920s or even Chartism. ... The new movement has sprouted out of the crevices of the working-class movement, at the points where new pressures have arisen in conflict with the traditional ideas of Labourism. Black people, women, socialist trade unionists, inner city tenants: these are some of the forces, disillusioned with Labour government and parliament, which have begun to organize on the edge of mainstream politics. ... What they have in common is a belief in their own ability to organize for change and a firm commitment to the value of education. (p. 174)

With a new constituency and new politics, radical adult educators have searched for theoretical constructs and explanations to describe the sociopolitical terrain and goals of the new social movements. Because the goals of these movements are not the seizure of state power, and their base is generally not considered to be the working class, radical adult educators have searched for and attempted to develop new theoretical tools to explain exactly where these movements operate and what exactly they do. To this end, they have revived the concept of civil society to explain the movements. Generally speaking, they argue that new social movements operate in civil society, which they define as social space between or outside the state and the economy. Furthermore, they argue, these movements democratize civil society and protect it from intrusions from the state and the economy. In developing this idea, many have evoked Antonio Gramsci's concept of civil society. This, I believe, is very problematic, because as a communist Gramsci was committed to and worked for the seizure of state power by the working class and the construction of a socialist society. In other words, radical adult educators who privilege new social movements are taking a theoretical construct—Gramsci's specific usage of civil society—from a socialist political strategy and attempting to use it to explain what in essence is a social democratic or radical pluralist strategy. Outside its intended framework, Gramsci's conception of civil society loses all meaningfulness; a more comprehensive explanation of this argument forms the basis of Chapter 5.

This emergence of social movement and civil society politics is the dominant paradigm in radical adult education today and will define the theory and practice of this area of the field for the near future. This study is an effort to engage this paradigm in debate and challenge its major assumptions. I am not alone in my skepticism of this new paradigm in radical adult education and radical politics in general. Throughout the study, I use a radical pluralist–socialist dichotomy to reflect the major division within the debate over this new paradigm. The radical pluralists, who also call themselves radical democrats or post-Marxists, advocate social movement and civil society politics as a fundamentally new and more authentic politics capable of significant social transformation in the contemporary era. The socialist perspective is generally skeptical of the political potential of social movements, arguing that on their own, new social movements tend to be temporary, largely middle class and therefore reformist, and easily co-opted by capitalist democracy.

I summarize, analyze, and critique this new paradigm in radical adult education in four ways that reflect the structure of the study. First, in Chapter 2, I present the major theories of the politics of social movements from radical pluralist and socialist perspectives. To place these perspectives in a wider context, I analyze the development of the sociology of social movements from which they have emerged. Although Chapter 2 deals with work outside the field of adult education, it is necessary to provide this context because, as we see in Chapter 4, adult educators draw on theories of the sociology and politics of social movements from outside the field in their analysis of the politics and nature of adult education within social movements. Second, Chapter 3 provides an analysis of major theories of civil society in what I call the Marxist tradition and beyond. I look at the major precursors to Karl Marx's conceptualization of civil society—John Locke, Adam Ferguson, and Georg Hegel, before analyzing Marx himself. I then look at three major theories of civil society after Marx: the work of Antonio Gramsci; the major contemporary radical pluralist perspective of Jean Cohen and Andrew Arato; and the major neo-Marxist perspective of John Keane. Third, Chapter 4 brings the politics of social movements and civil society together in an analysis of how this paradigm has taken shape in radical adult education. Fourth, I conclude the study with Chapter 5 by returning to Gramsci, alongside Paulo Freire, arguably the most influential theorist for radical adult educators today. In Chapter 5, I attempt to reconceptualize Gramsci's idea of civil society by showing how it cannot be understood outside his overall political project. I conclude the chapter by arguing that if we are to operate from a Gramscian perspective, we must take seriously his insistence upon the political party (an old social movement) as the fundamental organizational form to unite all the manifestations of resistance that confront us in our daily work as radical adult educators.

METHODOLOGY

Before we begin, it is important to describe the methodology I employ in my critique of contemporary conceptualizations of the politics of social movements and civil society in radical adult education. I base my critique on what I consider to be a classical Marxist position, which sees Marxism as a living and ongoing effort to understand and transcend capitalist relations.

Frederick Engels (1880/1989), Marx's intellectual companion of forty years, identified the two fundamentals of Marx's thinking: "these two great discoveries, the materialist conception of history and the revelation of the secret of capitalist production through surplus value, we owe to Marx" (p. 53). These discoveries are not unrelated, for Marx perceived the production of surplus value through his analysis of the dual character of a commodity as both use value and exchange value by studying capitalism historically, dialectically, and as a materialist. It is precisely the combination of these three forms of analysis that sets Marx apart as a thinker. Therefore, if one is to understand or use Marx's analysis, it is fundamental to understand how he viewed society from a dialectical, historical, and materialist perspective. Marx and Engels called this the *materialist conception of history* or, at times, *historical materialism*.

In this section I will outline Marx's materialist conception of history. To this end, I will begin, as Marx did, with Hegel's philosophical system and discuss what Marx and Engels saw as most important in Hegel's system. I will then show how Marx and Engels took the "rational kernel" of Hegel's system to develop historical materialism. Within the discussion of historical materialism, I will emphasize Marx and Engels' approach to the study of ideas and ideology, because this is largely the study of the current resurgence in theoretical work on the concept of civil society and the role of social movements therein. In short, through an analysis of Marx and Engels' historical materialism, I will begin to formulate a Marxist methodology for the study of current adult education theory of social change through social movements in civil society.

Marx's Hegelian Roots

Hegel's philosophy was a comprehensive system in that it offered an interpretation of the history and development of the world, both natural and human. Hegel's system included an analysis of the historical development of humanity, the role of philosophy and ideology, the nature of political formations, and the relation of all of this to nature. Hegel believed that what he called the "Idea" alienated itself and became its opposite—human, material existence. The history of humanity, and particularly reason and philosophy, is the overcoming of this alienation through the self-realization of the Idea in human history, culminating in the philosophical system of Hegel himself. Furthermore, Hegel rejuvenated the philosophical tool of dialectics as the fundamental principle of understanding change. Human history was a process in which the self-alienation of the Idea was overcome through the superseding of contradictions.

From this very brief sketch of Hegel, we see three aspects of his work that emerge very early in the writings of Marx and remain important to Marx throughout his lifetime. First, Marx realized the importance of understanding society as a totality in which various historical epochs emerge, develop, and are eventually superseded. Engels (1880/1989) captures the importance of Hegel's influence in this regard when he says, "In . . . [Hegel's] system—and herein is its great merit—for the first time the whole world, natural, historical, intellectual, is represented as a process, i.e., as in constant motion, change, transformation, development; and the attempt is made to trace out the internal connection that makes a continuous whole of all this movement in development" (p. 49). When Engels speaks of the world as a process in constant motion and transformation, he is referring to Hegel's dialectical view of society—the second major influence of Hegel on Marx. Marx (1867/1977a) was quick to point out, however, that his method of inquiry was "not only different from the Hegelian, but exactly opposite to it" (p. 102). That said, he was also equally forthright in acknowledging the fundamental debt he owed to Hegel for his dialectics. Marx says that Hegel was the first to present dialectics in "its general forms of motion in a comprehensive and conscious manner," and that once inverted, the dialectic became "critical and revolutionary" (p. 103). When Marx speaks of inverting Hegel, he is referring to the fact that while Hegel's historical and dialectical method makes possible, for the first time, a profound understanding of the world, his idealism obscures reality to a point where his method was, in the words of Engels, "unusable." We see how Marx, the materialist, differs from Hegel, the idealist, in their respective applications of the dialectic to an analysis of alienation—the third major area of influence of Hegel on Marx.

Of Hegel's idealist view of alienation, Marx (1977b) says that "he considers . . . wealth and the power of the state as beings alienated from man's being, this happens only in their conceptual form. . . . They are conceptual beings and thus simply an alienation of pure, i.e., abstract, philosophical thought. The whole process therefore ends with absolute knowledge" (p. 99). Therefore, in the years 1842–1843, when Marx, still under the heavy influence of Hegel's idealist dialectic, wrote for the newspaper *Rheinische Zeitung*, his "embarrassment of having to take part in discussions on so-called material interests" (Marx, 1977b, p. 388) revealed to him the inadequacy of Hegelian idealism for the study of concrete phenomena. Two years later, having moved to Paris, where he encountered French socialism and communism, Marx engaged in a critique of Hegel's system and began to develop, along with Engels, his materialist conception of history in earnest.

Dialectical Materialism: Foundation of the Materialist Conception of History

Marx and Engels met in Brussels in 1845 and set out to develop their worldview in opposition to then-current German philosophy. The result was *The German Ideology*, which is a polemic against Ludwig Feuerbach, Bruno Bauer, and Max Stirner and at the same time an effort by Marx and Engels to show how history should be studied from the perspective of dialectical materialism. Therefore, before we begin to discuss historical materialism, it is important to look first at its philosophical foundation: dialectical materialism.

Sayers (1980) argues that the dialectics of Marx and Engels consists of four fundamental principles. First, all things exist in relation to other things. An object or person cannot be known in isolation. It is only when we think of things in relation to others that they have meaning. Second, all things are in movement; they develop and change. The most rock-solid mountain, society, and people all have a history in which they emerge, change, and transform into something else. Third, all concrete things possess internal contradictions that are the driving force of change. For Marx, the nature of social change must be studied from this perspective. For example, in *The Holy Family* Marx (1977b) says that "proletariat and wealth are opposites; as such they form a single whole. They are both forms of the world of private property. The question is what place each occupies in the antithesis. . . . Within this antithesis the private owner is therefore the conservative side, the proletariat, the destructive side. From the former arises the action of preserving the antithesis, from the latter, that of annihilating it" (p. 134). Fourth, Sayers cautions us to realize that for Marx, dialectics is a method of inquiry, a starting point from which to investigate the social and natural world and not an a priori dogma. As Engels says in a letter to Conrad Schmidt, "our conception of history is above all a guide to study, not a lever for construction after the manner of the Hegelian. All history must be studied afresh" (Marx & Engels, 1959, p. 396). If we return to the previous quote from *The Holy Family*, we see that Marx views society dialectically, but the dialectic is not some mystical, deterministic force pushing history forward but the way in which things and people come into relations; it is the human agency (class struggle) characteristic of these relations that moves history. Marx, of course, would concretely examine and lay bare these relations in his subsequent political and economic studies.

As stated above, the dialectics of Marx were not idealist but materialist. In the *Economic and Philosophic Manuscripts of 1844*, Marx (1959) realized the potential of the Hegelian dialectic. "The outstanding thing in Hegel's . . . dialectic of negativity as the moving and generating principle is . . . that Hegel conceives the self-genesis of man as a process,

conceives objectification as a loss of the object, as alienation and as transcendence of this alienation; that he thus grasps the essence of *labor* and
comprehends objective man—true, because real man—as the outcome of
man's *own labor*" (p. 140). This for Marx is fundamental. Over and over
again Marx would stress the fact that we make our own history and our
own society—its productive forces and relations, political formations,
and ideology—through our practical activity, our labor. Moreover, in
capitalist society the products of our labor, the process of production,
our fellow workers, and nature itself all become alienated from us. The
problem with Hegel's analysis is that "in Hegel the negation of the negation is not the confirmation of true being through the negation of the
apparent being. It is the confirmation of apparent being or self-alienated
being in its denial. . . . Therefore, supersession plays a very particular
role in which negation and conservation are united. . . . This supersession
in thought that lets its object remain in reality believes it has really overcome it" (Marx, 1977b, p. 107). Clearly, the major ramification here is in
terms of social change. An idealist dialectic, and philosophy in general,
is wholly conservative, for change takes place in the realm of ideas and
not in the real, material world. In *The German Ideology*, where Marx and
Engels (1976) attack Hegelianism in the form of the idealism of their
Young Hegelian contemporaries, they insist on this point. "Since the
Young Hegelians consider conceptions, thoughts, ideas . . . to which they
attribute an independent existence, as the real chains of men . . . , it is
evident that the Young Hegelians have to fight only against these illusions of consciousness. . . . This demand to change consciousness
amounts to a demand to interpret the existing world in a different way.
. . . The Young Hegelian ideologists . . . are the staunchest conservatives"
(pp. 35–36).

    If, as Marx says in his now-famous eleventh thesis on Feuerbach, the
point of philosophy is not to merely interpret the world but to change
it, then an idealist dialectic, operating merely in the realm of ideas, was
inadequate for the task of philosophy. In discussing the development of
his and Marx's thinking, Engels says the following:

the separation from Hegelian philosophy was here also the result of a return to
the materialist standpoint. That means it was resolved to comprehend the real
world—nature and history—just as it presents itself to everyone who approaches
it free from preconceived idealist crotchets. It was decided mercilessly to sacrifice
every idealist crotchet which could not be brought into harmony with the facts
conceived in their own . . . interconnection. And materialism means nothing more
than this. (Marx & Engels, 1959, p. 225)

We see, then, that Marx and Engels insisted upon a dialectic that was
materialist. Of equal importance, it must be understood that the mate-

rialism of Marx and Engels was dialectic. On this latter point Engels discusses two major limitations of the materialism that he and Marx inherited from the eighteenth century. Note in this quote how Engels connects the development of philosophical thinking directly to the level of scientific understanding of an epoch.

The materialism of the last century was predominantly mechanical, because at that time, of all natural sciences only mechanics . . . of gravity had come to any definite close. . . . The second specific limitation of this materialism lay in its inability to comprehend the universe as a process, as matter undergoing uninterrupted historical development. This was in accordance with the level of the natural science of that time, and with the . . . antidialectical manner of philosophizing connected with it. (p. 211)

Therefore, Marx and Engels, "standing on the shoulders" of those who came before them (and acknowledging it as so), developed a new way of understanding existence: a materialist dialectic and a dialectical materialism. This is the famous inversion of Hegel. "We comprehended the concepts in our heads . . . materialistically as images of real things instead of regarding the real things as images of this or that stage of the absolute concepts. Thus dialectics reduced itself to the science of the general laws of motion, both of the external world and of human thought. . . . Thereby the dialectic of concepts itself became merely the conscious reflex of the dialectical motion of the real world" (Engels, in Marx & Engels, 1959, p. 226). This outlook, dialectical materialism, Engels called "our best working tool and our sharpest weapon" (p. 226). It is now only left to be seen how they applied this outlook to the study of history.

The Materialist Conception of History

An analysis of Marx and Engels' materialist conception of history must rely heavily on *The German Ideology*, for it was in this book, and particularly in Part I, where they set down in such detail for the first time their views on history and its proper study. We can begin with their premises on history, which they describe as "not arbitrary" and that therefore "can be verified in a purely empirical way" (Marx & Engels, 1976, pp. 36–37).

First, "men must be in a position to live in order to be able to 'make history'" (p. 47). The first historical act involves the satisfaction of basic needs such as food, clothing, and shelter—in other words, "the production of material life itself" (p. 47). Second, "the satisfaction of the first need . . . leads to new needs" (p. 48). Third, "men, who daily recreate their own life, begin to make other men, to propagate their kind: the relation between man and woman, parents and children, *the family*" (p.

48). From these first three circumstances that occur simultaneously and throughout history, they conclude that

the production of life, both of one's own in labor and of fresh life in procreation, now appears as a twofold relation: on the one hand as a natural, on the other as a social relation—social in the sense that it denotes the co-operation of several individuals. . . . It follows from this that a certain mode of production, or industrial stage, is always combined with a certain mode of co-operation, or social stage, and this mode of co-operation is itself a "productive force." (pp. 48–49)

Summarizing, they state that these "premises are men, not in fantastic isolation and fixity, but in their actual empirically perceptible process of development under definite conditions. As soon as this active life-process is described, history ceases to be a collection of dead facts, as it is with the empiricists . . . , or as imagined activity of imagined subjects as with the idealists" (p. 43). It is not enough to be empirical with the study of history—to have a perfect video-sound recording of history, so as to know the exact sequence of events—but one must draw out the relationship between these facts as well. Here we see the importance of the dialectic; one must see how historical change emerges from contradictions within a society. In the words of Marx and Engels, in a now-classic summation of historical materialism:

definite individuals who are productively active in a definite way enter into these definite social and political relations. Empirical observation must in each separate instance bring out empirically . . . the connection of the social and political structure with production. The social structure and the state are continually evolving out of the life-process of definite individuals, however, of these individuals not as they may appear in their own or other people's imagination, but as they *actually* are, i.e., as they act, produce materially, and hence as they work under definite material limits, presuppositions and conditions independent of their will. (p. 41)

The above quote contains Marx and Engels' method of analyzing consciousness, ideas, and philosophy. For to demonstrate the relationship between the social and political structure with production is to deal with the realm of ideas. It is important to keep in mind at this point that when Marx and Engels speak of production and productive relations, these are in their broadest conception. This is not to say, for example, only while we are at work, but the production of all that is necessary to produce and reproduce life and all the relations that we enter into in that process. "Consciousness" for Marx and Engels (1976) "can never be anything else than conscious being, and the being of men is their actual life process" (p. 42). Specifically addressing the nature of ideology and its relation to the life process, Marx and Engels say that "morality, religion, metaphysics, and all the rest of ideology as well as the forms of consciousness corresponding to these, thus no longer retain the semblance of independence. They have no history, no development; but men, developing their material production and their material intercourse, alter, along with this their actual world, also their thinking and products of their thinking. It is not consciousness that determines life, but life that determines consciousness" (p. 42). Our thinking is directly tied to our practical activity and the relations we enter into in this activity. As we change our world, we change our thinking about it. It must be kept in mind that this activity and relations are not abstractions but the definite empirically verifiable relations and actions of individuals of a particular historical juncture who inherit forces of production, knowledge, and ways of being from the past.

In his later years, after the death of Marx, Engels engaged in a series of correspondences with "Marxists" around the world in which he dealt specifically with the question of a historical materialist analysis of ideology. Historical materialism has often been criticized for being economic determinism, in that everything comes down to production and there is no role for ideology in the process of social change. This is a poor reading of Marx, to say the least, and Engels was well aware of these charges.

According to the materialist conception of history, the *ultimately* determining element in history is the production and reproduction of material life. More than this neither Marx nor I has ever asserted. Hence if somebody twists this into saying that the economic element is the *only* determining one he transforms that proposition into a . . . senseless phrase. The economic situation is the basis, but the various elements of the superstructure—political forms of the class struggle and its results, to wit: constitutions . . . , juridical forms, and even the reflexes of all these actual struggles in the brains of the participants, political, juristic, philosophical theories, religious views . . . also exercise their influence upon the course of historical struggles and in many cases preponderate in determining their *form*. (Engels, in Marx & Engels, 1959, pp. 397–398)

Indeed, how could it be otherwise? We know our own history. We know that long before we created states and political formations, we produced and reproduced material life. This is what shaped and continues to shape our views of ourselves and the world around us. As that process grew more complex, with the various divisions of labor that emerged, we developed for ourselves states, politics, and ideologies from the process of production. Of course these superstructural forms have a certain independence, but they are ultimately tied to the process of producing and reproducing life. In a letter to Conrad Schmidt, Engels provides a general outline of the study of seventeenth- and eighteenth-century philosophy from this perspective.

The people who attend to this [philosophy] belong . . . to a special sphere in the division of labor and appear to themselves to be working in an independent field. . . . Their productions . . . react upon the whole development of society, even on its economic development. But all the same, they themselves are in turn under the dominating influence of economic development. In philosophy, for instance . . . Hobbes was the first modern materialist . . . , but he was absolutist in a period [of] absolute monarchy. . . . Locke, both in religion and politics, was the child of the class compromise of 1688. The English deists and . . . the French materialists were the true philosophers of the bourgeoisie. . . . Here economy creates nothing anew, but it determines the way in which the thought material found in existence is altered and further developed, and that, too, for the most part indirectly, for it is the political, legal, and moral reflexes which exert the greatest direct influence in philosophy. (Marx and Engels, 1959, pp. 405–406)

If one is to study ideology, then one must demonstrate the relationship between ideology and politics and the changing nature of the relations of production. Embedded within the relations of production is the contradiction between labor and capital: class struggle. Fundamentally, class struggle, and the way that we conceive it, has, as always, taken on new characteristics. From a dialectical standpoint this would have to be the case, because from this perspective society is in constant motion and change. The task of the researcher is to articulate the exact changing nature of class struggle and the relationship of these changes to our conceptions of class struggle. Clearly, the whole notion of "old" versus "new" social movements is an example of this. Old social movements, such as unions and working-class political parties, are seen as obsolete by those who advocate new social movements precisely because of the perceived declining relevance of industrial production (the place of origin of old social movements) in the industrialized nations. Because new social movements do not directly operate in the realm of the economy, nor do they try to overthrow the state, theoreticians have rejuvenated the concept of civil society to understand the place of new social movements in society.

When Marx (1977b) realized that the working class was historically and socially situated to be the agent to overthrow capitalism and create a socialist society, he declared that "a philosophy finds in the proletariat its material weapons, so the proletariat finds in philosophy its intellectual weapons, and as soon as the lightning of thought has struck deep into the virgin soil of the people, the emancipation of the Germans into men will be complete" (p. 73). Clearly the radical pluralists have found their material weapons in new social movements. Their philosophy speaks to the ultimate aims of new social movements: bourgeois rights (autonomy) for petit-bourgeois elements.

2

The Sociology and Politics of Social Movements

Radical adult educators are more frequently looking to social movements as an important (Spencer, 1995; Welton, 1993), and at times, the fundamental (Finger, 1989; Holford, 1995) site for social change. This fact places these adult educators within an exponentially growing debate over the sociology, politics, and pedagogy of social movements. This debate is shaped by and forms a part of debates within Marxism over theories of the state and civil society, the debate over the current nature of the working class, and the impact of postmodernism on theory and social action. Because this literature on social movements is literally overwhelming in size and scope, the focus here will be primarily on what I call the politics of social movements. I believe that it is appropriate to focus primarily on the politics of social movements because adult educators look to social movements for what they see as their social change potential much more than as a way to understand society generally. The latter is what I call *social movement theory*, or, more specifically, social movements as a theoretical construct within sociology to understand human behavior and social relations. To place the relevant literature on the politics of social movements in proper context, however, I will begin with a review of the major currents of social movement theory within sociology.

THE SOCIOLOGY OF SOCIAL MOVEMENTS

Garner (1997), using the work of Kuhn (1970) on paradigms in the sciences, argues that there have been three periods and corresponding paradigms in the history of social movement theory. The first period is the 1940s and 1950s, which were characterized by a negative view of social movements and a heavy reliance on social psychological analysis. The 1960s and 1970s, the second period, witnessed a paradigm shift toward a positive view of social movements and the use of macrosociological analysis. We are currently in the third period, argues Garner, which she characterizes as a period of "deconstruction" because of the influence of postmodernism in social movement analysis. Although I agree with Garner's analysis of the shifting paradigms and periodization of social movement theory since the 1940s, social movement theory—or collective behavior theory, as it was more commonly called before the 1960s—did not begin in the 1940s. At least as far back as the late 1920s, Jerome Davis was teaching a semester-long course on social movements at Yale University (Davis, 1930, p. ix), as was J. Stewart Burgess at Temple University beginning in the late 1930s (Burgess, 1944, p. 271). The fact that a Barnes & Noble popular college outline, *An Outline of the Principles of Sociology*, first published in 1939, includes a chapter by Blumer (1939) on collective behavior is further evidence that there was already wide institutional interest in social movements and collective behavior in academia in the 1930s. Moreover, the term *collective behavior* was coined by Robert Park in the early 1920s (Turner & Killian, 1957, p. 7), and the term *social movements* was in use as far back as the early nineteenth century (Heberle, 1968, p. 439). Indeed, most social movement theorists see Gustave LeBon as the "founder" (Turner & Killian, 1957, p. 5) or "grandfather" (Berk, 1974, p. 20) of the field with his book *The Crowd*, first published in 1896.

Even choosing LeBon as the founder of social movement theory is somewhat arbitrary, given the fact that others before him wrote on social movements, yet it is not without ideological significance. For as Turner and Killian (1957) indicate, the work of pioneers in sociology such as Auguste Comte, Herbert Spencer, and Emile Durkheim do address collective behavior (p. 4), and—more important, I would argue—scholars such as Lorenz von Stein (1850/1964) and Marx wrote directly on social movements. Lorenz von Stein's book *Die Geschichte der Sozialen Bewegung in Frakreich von 1789 bis auf unsere Tage*, translated as *The History of the Social Movement in France, 1789–1850*, published in 1850, analyzes the movement of the working class in France, which he calls *the* social movement, yet this work is ignored as an early contribution to social movement theory. More disturbing still is the neglect of Marx's work—*The Communist Manifesto, Class Struggles in France, The 18th Brumaire of Louis Bonaparte*, and *The Civil War in France*, to name only a few of his contributions. Ideologically, to begin with, LeBon does highlight the ironically reactionary nature of much of the early literature on social movements and collective behavior within academia. For, as we shall see, LeBon represents an anti–working-class, conservative perspective that attempts to put research into the service of those social forces striving to maintain class power and privilege. LeBon's ideological perspective that sees working-class social movements as irrational behavior, with notable exceptions (Davis, 1930; Katz, 1940; LaPiere, 1938; Maier, 1942), is, as Garner (1997) argues, the dominant paradigm at least until the 1950s.

Given the heavy influence of LeBon on the field of social movement theory, I will begin a survey of the sociology of social movements with an analysis of his most famous work, *The Crowd*. My analysis of LeBon and subsequent theorists will follow the methodological perspectives outlined in Chapter 1 and will focus on the historical context and class location of the author. A recurring theme in the history of social movement theory is the impact on this theory of the social movements of the period in which a theorist writes. This fact could not be more clear with LeBon and William McDougall. In the latter periods of social movement theory, we will see how social movements have an opposite effect on theorists who are increasingly sympathetic, or at least not hostile, to progressive social movements. After an analysis of the early sociology of social movements, the period beginning with LeBon, I will use Garner's periodization in my survey of the later sociology of social movements and analyze a few exemplary theorists of each period.

The Early Sociology of Social Movements

Gustave LeBon

Gustave LeBon, writing *The Crowd* in France in the 1890s, faced a world undergoing tremendous change. Many have commented (e.g., Hayes, 1941; Swart, 1964) on the ambivalence facing ruling-class intellectuals like LeBon at the time. Advances in science were arming them with the tools, methodology, and vocabulary to analyze and understand the natural and social world as no time before ever had, and yet they confronted the emergence of a powerful working-class mass at odds with the society they hoped to improve through the application of science. LeBon makes this emerging working class central to his purpose in analyzing the nature and behavior of crowds. In the introduction of *The Crowd*, LeBon (1896) says, "The present epoch is one of these critical moments in which the thought of mankind is undergoing a process of transformation. . . . On whatever lines the societies of the future are organized, they will have to count with a new power, . . . the power of crowds. . . . Scarcely a century ago . . . the opinion of the masses scarcely counted at all. To-day . . . the voice of the masses has become preponderant" (pp. 14–15). Early on, and throughout the work as well, we see how LeBon is preoccupied by "the masses" in his study of crowds. Specifically, what worries LeBon is the fact that "the masses are founding syndicates . . . ; they are founding labor unions. . . . Today the claims of the masses are becoming more and more sharply defined, and amount to nothing less than a determination to utterly destroy society as it now exists, with a view to making it hark back to that primitive communism" (p. 16). For LeBon, it is imperative to understand the crowd, and particularly the masses formed into crowds, in order that society may prevent its own destruction. *The Crowd* in some senses reads as a nineteenth-century French version of Niccolo Machiavelli's *The Prince*, in that LeBon warns and advises the ruling classes of his day about the nature and direction of "the popular mind" (see Moscovici, 1985). In the introduction LeBon notes, "It is possible that the advent to power of the masses marks one of the last signs of Western civilization. . . . But may this result be prevented?" (p. 18). To the politician he remarks, "A knowledge of the psychology of crowds is to-day the last resource of the statesman who wishes not to . . . be too much governed by them" (p. 21). In no way, it should be added, is LeBon alone in this endeavor. As Swart (1964) argues, "throughout the nineteenth century, from Joseph de Maistre to Charles Maurras, the revolutionary principles remained the main target of French conservatives. Numerous French scholars such as Tocqueville, LePlay, Renan, Taine, and Gustave LeBon pioneered in the study of democratic and revolutionary movements and were instrumental in strengthening the intellectuals of other countries in their abhorrence of political equalitarianism" (p. 257).

Before we continue with an analysis of the historical context in which LeBon writes and the relationship between this context and the ideological approach of his work, it is important to turn to a summary of the main contents of his book: the psychology of crowds. In critiquing his analysis of the psychology of crowds, I will revisit the relationship of his ideas to the historical juncture in which he writes.

LeBon (1896) begins by defining crowds. He says, "Under certain given circumstances, and only under those circumstances, an agglomeration of men presents new characteristics very different from those of the individuals composing it. . . . A collective mind is formed. . . . It forms a single being, and is subjected to the *law of the mental unity of crowds*" (p. 26). He calls this a *psychological crowd*. He points out that physical proximity is not a prerequisite for the formation of a psychological crowd. "Thousands of isolated individuals may acquire at certain moments . . . the characteristics of a psychological crowd" (p. 27). LeBon detests what he considers to be the stupefaction of the individual within a psychological crowd. "By the mere fact that he forms part of an organized crowd, a man descends several rungs in the ladder of civilization. Isolated, he may be a cultivated individual; in a crowd, he is a barbarian" (p. 36). Continuing, he summarizes the psychology of the individual within a crowd. "The disappearance of the conscious personality, the predominance of the unconscious personality, the turning by means of suggestion and contagion of feelings and ideas in an identical direction, the tendency to immediately transform the suggested ideas into acts; these we see are the principal characteristics of the individual forming a part of a crowd" (p. 37). Because individuals lose their ability for any independent rational thought within a crowd, they easily fall victim to the prestige of leaders who use affirmation, repetition, and contagion to impress images upon the collective mind of a crowd that spur the crowd to act.

Undergirding LeBon's analysis are the social Darwinist theories of race prevalent in the latter part of the nineteenth century that emerge and grow along with European and U.S. imperialism. In fact, in detailing what he calls the "remote factors" that determine the opinions of crowds, LeBon says that "race . . . must be placed in the first rank, for in itself it far surpasses in importance all the others" (p. 91), such as tradition, time, institutions, and education. Moreover, race is the *fundamental* factor determining the beliefs held by a crowd. LeBon argues that there are two types of beliefs held by crowds: transitory and fixed. Transitory beliefs are easily changeable, although they may last up to a generation. Of these transitory beliefs, he says, "the opinions which are not linked to any general belief or sentiment of the race . . . are always momentary" (p. 169). Fixed beliefs, on the other hand, are rooted in the characteristics of the race. From these beliefs, societal institutions are built and can only be destroyed through violent revolution.

The Crowd is not the first work in which LeBon espouses his racial theory. His previous book, *The Psychology of Peoples*, provides a book-length treatment of his theory of race in which LeBon (1894/1974) says, "The human race may be divided into four groups: (1) the primitive races; (2) the inferior races; (3) the average races; (4) the superior races" (pp. 26–27). He places Fuegians and aboriginal Australians in the category of primitive; Negroes, he says, are most representative of the inferior races; Chinese, Japanese, Mongolians, and Semitic people are average races; and "only Indo-European peoples can be classed among the superior races" (p. 27).

LeBon's "psychology" of crowds and races is illustrative of the French bourgeois class outlook of the latter half of the nineteenth century. Hayes (1941) argues that European nationalist thought was transformed in the mid-nineteenth century from what he calls a liberal nationalism to a nascent totalitarian nationalism.

All sorts of earlier nationalists had talked much about "race," but their talk had usually been loose and literary and without pretense to scientific exactitude. . . . A change came with the vogue of social Darwinism after the national struggles of the [18]60s and [18]70s. Obviously the "fittest" nations "survived." But what made a nation "fittest"? Social scientists, becoming obsessed with the transcendent importance of heredity, jumped to the conclusion that it must be the one whose biological racial stock was best. (pp. 255–256)

In discussing the same phenomenon, Marx (1867/1977a) says the following:

In France and England the bourgeoisie had conquered political power. From that time on, the class struggle took on more and more explicit and threatening form, both in practice and theory. . . . In place of disinterested inquirers there stepped hired prize-fighters; in place of genuine scientific research, the bad conscience and evil intent of apologetics. (p. 97)

Indeed, there can be no doubt that LeBon was a "prize-fighter" for the bourgeoisie of his day. In fact, he actively promoted himself as such in his weekly luncheon seminars to this very class (Clark, 1984, p. 135). His race theory justifies the expansion of European imperialism in the latter half of the nineteenth century, and his psychology of crowds justifies the continued rule by force of the bourgeoisie when faced with the "era of crowds."

LeBon is important in the history of social movement theory. Although his work is limited by its pseudoscientific methodology, which uses a scientific discourse to make up for a total lack of scientific method, and by its Machiavellian intentions, which bias the work beyond scholarly utility, it has nevertheless had a wide impact on the field. His ideas are taken up by prominent successors in the field (Christensen, 1915; Conway, 1915; Martin, 1923; Ross, 1916; Trotter, 1919), of which one of the most important is William McDougall.

William McDougall

William McDougall was born into a northern English manufacturing family in 1871. He says that "northern manufacturers were a class apart from the rest of the English social system. They were class-conscious, conscious of power and of their peculiar interests" (McDougall, 1961, p. 193). In McDougall's 1920 book, *The Group Mind*, we can see the continuation of LeBon's work on collective behavior, race, and nationality. While McDougall's work parallels that of LeBon in many areas, there is an interesting nuance that McDougall adds to his perspective on collective behavior. On the one hand, both McDougall and LeBon reflect the reactionary nature of early social movement theory. Both fear and loathe the working class and its organizations, and both subscribe to and advocate a white-supremacist ideology that openly justifies imperialism. On the other hand, however, McDougall realizes that if one condemns collective behavior outright, one condemns the notion of civilization and modern nation-states—the products of his bourgeois class's own collective behavior. McDougall (1920) calls this problem a paradox. "Participation in group life degrades the individual, assimilating his mental processes to those of the crowd, whose brutality, inconstancy, and unreasoning impulsiveness have been the theme of many writers; yet only by participation in group life does man become fully man, only so does he rise above the level of the savage" (pp. 27–28). We will see, then, how McDougall is able to condemn working-class collective behavior while advocating that of the bourgeoisie.

The subtitle of *The Group Mind*, "A Sketch of the Principles of Collective Psychology with Some Attempt to Apply Them to the Interpretation of National Life and Character," summarizes McDougall's project. He opens the work with five chapters on collective psychology, followed by fifteen chapters relating collective psychology to the nation-state, nationality, and the concept of race. The first five chapters are important for this study; nevertheless, I will also critique his concepts of race and nationality because they reveal most clearly his class perspective.

Like LeBon, McDougall (1920) begins with the premise that a group has a mentality that is greater than the sum of its parts. He says, "The social aggregate has a collective mental life, which is not merely the sum of the mental lives of its units" (p. 10). Moreover, LeBon and McDougall converge on their condemnation of the crowd. McDougall "fully recognizes the mental and moral defects of the crowd and its degrading effects upon all those who are caught up in it and carried away by the contagion of its reckless spirit" (p. 28). We also see that McDougall has a particular social group in mind when he discusses crowd behavior. He argues that an addiction to the excitement of crowd behavior can develop. "The repeated enjoyment of effects of this kind tends to generate a craving for them . . . ; this is probably the principal cause of the greater excitability of urban populations . . . and of the well-known violence and fickleness of the mobs of great cities" (p. 35). His analysis of the degrading effects of crowd behavior are aimed particularly at urban crowds. McDougall summarizes his analysis of the crowd with the following statement, which deserves to be quoted at length to show the full extent of his loathing of urban crowds. He says that the crowd is

excessively emotional, impulsive, violent, fickle, inconsistent, irresolute and extreme in action, displaying only the coarse-emotions and less refined sentiments; extremely suggestible, careless in deliberation, hasty in judgement, incapable of any but the simpler and imperfect forms of reasoning; easily swayed and led, lacking in self-consciousness, devoid of self respect and of responsibility, and apt to be carried away by the consciousness of its own force, so that it lends to produce all the manifestations we have learnt to expect of any irresponsible and absolute power. Hence its behavior is like that of an unruly child or an untutored passionate savage in a strange situation. (p. 64)

After discussing crowds, McDougall moves on to discuss groups of a higher level, of which he says there are two major types, natural and artificial. Natural groups consist of those based on kinship and those based on geography—of which the nation is the focus for McDougall. He argues that "better kinds of organization render group life the great enabling influence" (p. 28). Of this type of organization, McDougall points to the nation-state as "the most interesting, most complex, and most important kind of group mind" (p. 135).

It could be argued that at the opening of McDougall's discussion of the nation-state, he has moved beyond the terrain of collective behavior; he himself does not believe so, and he argues that the nation-state is a form of collective behavior with a group mind of the highest order. To understand nations and nationhood, moreover, one must understand and utilize the concept of group mind, for nations are foremost mental organizations. What has plagued other scholars in defining nationhood is precisely "organization; not material organization, but such mental organization as will render the group capable of effective group life, of collective deliberation and collective volition. The answer to the riddle of the definition of nationhood is to be found in the conception of the group mind" (p. 141).

Having defined nations as principally psychological organizational entities, McDougall then makes the leap to scientific racism to explain asymmetrical power and economic relations between nations. "Individual psychology tends more and more to be a genetic psychology; because we do not feel that we really understand the individual mind, . . . until we know something of its development and racial evolution. Just so the explanatory psychology of peoples must be a genetic psychology. Here it differs from individual psychology in that the distinction between individual development and racial evolution disappears" (p. 147). This allows McDougall to claim that "the social environment in a developed nation [read: any formed and recognized nation, not *developed* as we use that term today] is in harmony with the individual innate tendencies, because in the main it is the natural outcome and expression of these tendencies" (p. 156). So, for example, the problems facing a nation such as Haiti, which he cites as proof of the inferiority of the Negro race (p. 163), have nothing to do with imperialism but with the racial characteristics of Negroes, such as "the happy-go-lucky disposition, the unrestrained emotional violence and responsiveness" (p. 155).

Interestingly, McDougall is intellectually honest enough to admit that the question of the relationship between race and nationality is widely disputed and wholly lacking in research. "In considering racial or native homogeneity, we touch upon one aspect of a much disputed question, the influence of race on national character and history, in regard to which the greatest diversity of opinion has prevailed and still prevails" (p. 150).

Specifically, regarding research and the questions of race and nationality, he says, "They admit of no clear answers at the present time . . . and only when prolonged research shall have been directed to them shall we be able to answer them positively" (pp. 153–154). This does not stop him, however, from devoting thirteen more chapters to showing how race is a primary factor in a nation's group mind and destiny.

McDougall's scientific racism forms part of a larger white-supremacist, anti-working-class movement among bourgeois intellectuals going back to at least the 1850s and Joseph Arthur de Gobineau's *The Inequality of the Races.* Of Gobineau, Finot (1906) says that he "never attempted to dissimulate the motive which led him to write his *Essai.* For him indeed it was only a matter of bringing his contributions to the great struggle against equality and the emancipation of the proletariat" (p. 7). Chase (1977) echoes this argument when he says, "Bigotry is not one of the functions of scientific racism; it is merely a later adjunct in the further-ance of the basic socioeconomic function of scientific racism" (p. xvi). This socioeconomic function is to justify the continued "greed, selfishness and poverty" of the bourgeois order. This "later adjunct" takes the form of eugenics in the early twentieth century. McDougall was a leader in the eugenics movement. In 1921, a year after *The Group Mind* was pub-lished, McDougall gave a series of lectures at the Lowell Institute in Boston promoting the eugenics movement. In these lectures McDougall (1921/1977) states that "an effective social ladder in any nation is a most important agency for the advancement of its civilization" (p. 151) be-cause "the social ladder tends to concentrate the valuable qualities of the whole nation in the upper strata, and to leave the lowest strata depleted of the finer qualities" (p. 155). The goal of eugenics is to "favor increase of the birth-rate among the intrinsically better part of the population, and its decrease among the inferior part" (p. 192).

For both McDougall and LeBon, the study of collective behavior was part of a larger anti–working-class project to provide the intellectual and "scientific" justifications for the bourgeois order. The political move-ments of the working class in their respective time periods and nations threatened the class interests of the bourgeois class these men defended. The most threatening manifestations of these working-class movements took the form of crowd or mass action—particularly in the urban areas of Paris, England, and the United States. McDougall and LeBon were not interested in the socioeconomic conditions that led to such action; an analysis of those causes would expose the inequalities of the bourgeois order and provide a justification for working-class movements. Rather, they looked to psychology and race theories to build a pseudoscience of collective behavior that condemned working-class collective action while justifying that of the bourgeoisie: social engineering eugenics at home and imperialism abroad.

Mass Society Theorists

Mass society theory is a current that runs through what I am calling the period of the "early sociology of social movements" through Garner's "first period." Mass-based proletarian and fascist movements and the alienation and "decline" resulting from world wars are the major concerns of mass society theorists. As a segue to the first period of social movement theory, I will examine Ortega y Gasset's *The Revolt of the Masses*.

José Ortega y Gasset

José Ortega y Gasset's *The Revolt of the Masses* is representative of the mass society theories that emerged in the 1930s and 1940s, which should be mentioned because they deal directly with collective behavior. An analysis of *The Revolt of the Masses* will provide us with a clear picture of the class perspective dominant in the mass society literature.

Dobson (1989) most succinctly summarizes Ortega y Gasset's theoretical predicament in *The Revolt of the Masses*. Ortega y Gasset was "a bourgeois, liberal thinker historically, socially and politically squeezed between the demands of an organized working class and newly fledged corporate solutions to the crisis of capitalism" (p. 105). Indeed, Ortega y Gasset wrote *The Revolt of the Masses* in the late 1920s in a Spain that was witnessing intense class struggle. As Dolores Ibarruri (1966), then a leader of the Spanish Communist Party, relates, "With the October Revolution, the revolutionary temper in Spain mounted; it spread to various social levels; from the industrial regions it extended and took hold in farming districts" (p. 67). This intense level of working-class activity continued through the dictatorship of General Miguel Primo de Rivera from 1923 to 1930. Coupled with working-class activity was the Republican movement's opposition to the continued power of the Spanish monarchy, which was not overthrown until the establishment of the republic in 1931. In addition, what Dobson refers to in the above quote as "corporate solutions" is primarily the emergence of fascism, which was taking hold in Spain at this very time. In brief, the Spanish working class, albeit plagued by serious rivalry among socialists, communists, and anarchists, was highly organized and taking the offensive; fascism as a response to the movement of the working class was growing; and Ortega y Gasset's bourgeois class was continuing its refusal to "carry out its own revolution—the democratic [bourgeois] revolution" (Ibarruri, 1966, p. 89). Within this context, let us now turn to an analysis of Ortega y Gasset's appraisal of the situation and his political project for the future of Spain as presented in *The Revolt of the Masses*.

The provocative title compels us to first look at how Ortega y Gasset defines *the masses* and the nature of their revolt. For Ortega y Gasset (1932/1960), the most fundamental division of society

is that which splits it into two classes of creatures: those who make great demands on themselves . . . ; and those who demand nothing special of themselves. . . . The division of society into masses and select minorities is, then, not a division into social classes, but into classes of men, and cannot coincide with the hierarchic separation of "upper" and "lower" classes. It is, of course, plain that in these "upper" classes . . . there is much more likelihood of finding men who adopt the "great vehicle," whereas the "lower" classes normally comprise individuals of minus quality. But, strictly speaking, within both of these social classes, there are to be found mass and genuine minority. (pp. 15–16)

Furthermore, because the masses, "by definition, neither should nor can . . . rule society" (p. 11), for "the masses to claim the right to act of itself is then a rebellion against its own destiny" (p. 116), and this for Ortega y Gasset is the nature of the revolt of the masses.

One is tempted, throughout the text, to come to Ortega y Gasset's defense against the obvious charge of elitism by countering that he is merely protesting mediocrity in all social classes, yet the overwhelming evidence of his writing and his political practice weigh on the side of elitism. Practically, while Ortega y Gasset flirted with socialism in the early part of the century and supported the republic for approximately its first two years, he also supported the dictatorship of Primo de Rivera until 1929 and did not oppose Francisco Franco "until . . . he came face to face with the regime on the first of his visits to Spain in 1945" (Dobson, 1989, p. 37). Conversely, it would also not be accurate to label him a fascist, even though later Spanish fascists would use his work, for Ortega y Gasset (1932/1960) was a liberal thinker:

Liberalism . . . is the supreme form of generosity; it is the right which the majority concedes to minorities and hence it is the noblest cry that has ever resounded [on] this planet. It announces the determination to share existence with the enemy; more than that, with an enemy which is weak. It was incredible that the human species should have arrived at so noble an attitude. . . . Hence it is not to be wondered at that this same humanity should soon appear anxious to get rid of it. (p. 76)

Indeed, it is incredible that humanity reached the economic and political level of eighteenth- and nineteenth-century liberalism that Ortega y Gasset praises and wishes to solidify in early twentieth-century Spain. The class-conscious working class believed that society had reached an even greater stage by the twentieth century that allowed for a qualitative change in the social order. Therefore, Ortega y Gasset's world turned upside down by the unworthy masses clamoring for leadership was, for the working class, the placing of the world right side up. Ortega y Gasset admitted the undeniable advances made in the accumulation of "man's worldly goods"; "the rule of the masses, then, presents a favorable aspect, inasmuch as it signifies an all-around rise in the historical level, and reveals that average existence to-day moves on a higher altitude" (p. 28). While Ortega y Gasset claimed that "mass-man believes that the civilization into which he was born and which he makes use of is as spontaneous and self-producing as Nature" (p. 89), the working class of Spain and many other industrializing nations of the time, armed with socialist ideology, were beginning to understand quite clearly that they had "built the seven towers of Thebes," and that it was time for an end to private accumulation of the social surplus they were most responsible for creating. The working class saw the possibility of this qualitative change as a reality with the events in Russia in 1917. Ortega y Gasset's class position, notwithstanding his early flirtation with socialism, did not allow him to see this new opening. "What has happened in Russia possesses no historic interest, it is . . . anything but a new start in human life" (p. 93).

Ortega y Gasset's political ideology can seem contradictory and hard to pin down if one considers that he sporadically supported a socialist-influenced Spanish Republic and the fascist dictatorships of Primo de Rivera and Franco. If one understands his political project as creating a bourgeois democratic Spain, however, then one sees how he is progressive in his support of the republic against the Spanish monarchy and reactionary in his support of dictatorships against working-class socialism. Similarly, therefore, Ortega y Gasset's *Revolt of the Masses* can at best be seen as a critique of the mediocrity of the petit bourgeois whose whole "ambition is reduced to hoping that each day is as identical as possible to all the others" (Ortega y Gasset, in Dobson, 1989, p. 52) and at worst, a justification to maintain the class privilege of his bourgeois class against the "rule of the masses."

The First Period of the Sociology of Social Movements

As stated above, Garner's (1997) "first period" of the sociology of social movements ranges roughly from the 1940s into the 1950s. Although I have argued that the sociology of social movements begins before this "first" period, and the studies I have discussed above show that social movements were a topic of research and study before the 1940s, the field does begin to really take shape in the 1940s. Evidence of this fact are the numerous articles throughout the 1940s that assess, albeit negatively, the field of collective behavior or social movement theory. Strauss (1944, 1947), Glick (1948), and Heberle (1949) all lament the lack of "systematic" research in the study of collective behavior. Meadows (1943), on the other hand, argues that a sufficient number of studies have been done on collective behavior, but the field lacks good theory. Wirth (1940) insists that the study of collective behavior would be improved with a focus on the ideological aspects of collective behavior. All of these studies show that the field is beginning to take shape and that theorists are grappling with ways to assess and improve the field. What distinguishes this period of social movement theory, however, is the dominant paradigm that sees collective behavior as ultimately irrational. In assessing this period I will focus on two theorists, Robert Park and Hadley Cantril, who strive to break away from this paradigm and in some ways do, yet ultimately do not provide a forthright challenge to it.

Robert Park

The work of Robert Park looms large in the sociology of social movements. In fact, as stated above, he is credited with coining the term *collective behavior*. A major reason for Park's dominant presence in the sociology of social movements is that his career extends from the time of what I call the early sociology of social movements through the post–World War II first period of Garner's periodization. Moreover, in terms of perspective on social movements, we can even say that Park's work reaches all the way to what Garner calls the second period of social movement theory, which is the 1960s and 1970s, and looks at social movements as rational agents of reform and structural change—an idea that we see is implicit, though in nascent form, in Park's *The Crowd and the Public* of 1904.

The Crowd and the Public is Park's doctoral dissertation and first work in the yet-to-be-named field of collective behavior. Park largely accepts the analysis of LeBon on the nature of crowds, yet his awareness of the overt class bias in LeBon's work propels him to expand on previous work by adding an analysis of *the public*. "Despite his acceptance of the LeBon-Sighele portrayal of crowd behavior, however, Park's inclusion of the public within the category of change-inducing groups radically altered the thrust of their tradition, for an irrational mechanism of change is now balanced by a mechanism that is rational and reasonable" (Elsner, 1972, p. xv).

In *The Crowd and the Public*, Park argues that there are two major categories of groups in society. The first group we can say is *institutionalized*—a term Park himself will use in later work (1939) to refer to the same type of group—and the second group is composed of much more temporary associations that include crowds and the public.

First, there is the category of sects, castes, classes, and groups which serve any special purpose whatsoever.... The only characteristic they have in common is that they are not isolated, or in existence only for themselves.... A political party, for example, assumes the existence of other political parties. . . . But the political parties . . . presume the existence of a collectivity in which they are viewed as the parts. Their aims and the forces which influence them are only the particular manifestations of a general will which attains fuller expression in the political organization of a state. . . . Crowd and public . . . represent the second type of association, which grows out of and beyond the others, and they serve to bring individuals out of old ties and into new ones. . . . The historical element . . . is partially or completely absent for the crowd as well as the public. Instead, the crowd and the public reveal the processes through which new groups are formed, although they are not yet conscious of themselves as groups. . . . They have no basis for viewing themselves as a permanent collectivity. (Park, 1904/1972, p. 78)

Park goes on to make the following distinctions between *the crowd* and *the public.*

Entrance to the crowd depends on the simplest conditions imaginable, namely, possessing the ability to feel and empathize. . . . The conditions under which one enters the public are somewhat more exacting. Not only the ability to feel and empathize is required, but also the ability to think and reason with others. . . . There is another difference between crowd and public: the public expresses criticism. Within the public, opinions are divided. When the public ceases to be critical, it dissolves or is transformed into a crowd. This provides the essential characteristic differentiating the crowd and the public: The crowd submits to the influence of the collective drive, which it obeys without criticism. The public, in contrast—precisely because it is composed of individuals with different opinions—is guided by prudence and rational reflection. (p. 80)

In the above quotes, we can see Park assimilating the previous work on crowds and moving beyond its class bias. Whereas LeBon and Mc-Dougall provide a shameless pseudoscientific assault on working-class organization and power, Park attempts to analyze the nature of change in society and through this process begin the development of a "theory of history." His theory of history, however, is weak. This is apparent in "The General Will" chapter of *The Crowd and the Public*, in which Park jumps from David Hume to John Locke to Thomas Hobbes to Georg Hegel to Jean-Jacques Rousseau and back again, desperately seeking an adequate explanation of the historical development of norms, which his ideas on public opinion do not adequately address. He says, "What is lacking is the recognition of practical norms—the acceptance of law" (pp. 61–62). He remains unsatisfied with all the aforementioned philosophers and leaves the question of how to study the general will, or norms, unanswered (p. 74).

In at least three ways, Park's work in *The Crowd and the Public* can be seen as a bridge from the blatantly class-biased work of crowd theorists to the first period of social movement theory. First, as stated earlier, although Park makes the crowd a major part of his analysis, he places the crowd within a broader analysis of social change that includes the notions of various forms of social association. Second, one form of association that Park analyzes, the public, is seen by him as being a rational, critical actor. The notion of associated, rational actors is a theme that begins to hold sway in the post–World War II period of social movement theory. Third, Park begins to place collective action within a more general theory of history. Rather than identifying incidents of irrational behavior such as crowds, mobs, or panic, Park is beginning to analyze the role of associated groups in forming and transforming society. Again, this is an approach that we will see in later works in the sociology of social movements.

Hadley Cantril

The work of Hadley Cantril, like that of Park, spans the various periods of the sociology of social movements. First, in terms of the political perspective of theorists toward social movements, Cantril can be seen as transitional between the first and second periods of the sociology of social movements. Second, despite his political perspective, his work—in terms of its ultimately psychologistic stigmatization of social movement leaders and participants as lacking critical ability—reaches all the way back to LeBon. Finally, his insistence that many of the questions regarding individual participation in social movements can only be answered by the social psychologist anticipates that of Klandermans (1997).

We can first look at how Cantril advances social movement theory through his emphasis on the social context in individual development, which openly rejects the theories of McDougall and Sigmund Freud, which were founded on theories of innate characteristics and drives. Conversely, we can see the limitations of Cantril in his inability to move beyond the then-dominant paradigm of social movement participation as irrational behavior.

In analyzing the mental context of individuals in social movements, Cantril (1941) says that "we must always look first at the particular pattern of norms which surround the individuals who compose that particular movement . . . if we are to avoid oversimplified solutions in terms of innate racial, sex, or class differences or in terms of instincts, or uniform urges, that are supposed to drive men to certain types of social behavior" (pp. 4–5). For Cantril, each individual has a mental context that is largely shaped by the society in which he or she lives. The mental context has three characteristics. The broadest characteristic is what he calls *standards of judgment*. These are very general values, preexisting in society, that we learn at an early age. These include notions of right and wrong, for example, from which we form the second characteristic of our

mental context: *frames of reference*. A frame of reference is a world outlook or what we might call "ideology." Our frames of reference shape
our *attitudes*, the third characteristic of our mental context. Cantril defines attitudes as interpretations of definite situations. Having defined
the mental context, Cantril then discusses motivation for behavior in
terms of the mental context and ego, which he defines as "what each
person subjectively regards as *me*" (p. 41). By using the concepts *ego
drive, self-regard*, and *status*, Cantril attempts to demonstrate how the
ego is largely made up of socially derived values as outlined in his
idea of a mental context. He says that the individual ego can come
into conflict with the social environment because "an individual is constantly trying to maintain or enhance his own feeling of self-regard"
(p. 46). He lists four sources of discontent arising from this conflict: (a)
a discrepancy between ego level and achievement level; (b) a state in
which status or values are not properly recognized by others; (c) a
state in which one cannot satisfy innate or acquired needs and maintain one's values; and (d) the failure of society to recognize certain values that an individual cherishes. These sources of discontent can lead
to what Cantril calls *critical situations*: "when an individual is confronted by a chaotic external environment which he cannot interpret
and which he wants to interpret" (p. 63).

Up to this point Cantril appears to be advancing past what he himself calls "oversimplified" theories that discuss motivation and behavior in terms of innate characteristics or reinforcement. Yet, it is
precisely at this moment that Cantril fails to go beyond the dominant
paradigm of his time. He argues that critical situations lead to the psychological condition of suggestibility. "It is these critical situations that
furnish fertile soil for the emergence of the mob leader, the potential
dictator, the revolutionary or religious prophet, or others with new
and untried formulae. Such leaders arise because they provide people
with an interpretation that brings order into their confused psychological worlds" (p. 66). Furthermore, those not subject to suggestibility,
and therefore participation in social movements, have what Cantril
calls *critical ability*. This is the opposite of suggestibility and is characterized by an adequate mental context for interpreting events or, if not
an adequate mental context, at least a readiness to question interpretations (p. 76). One can conclude from Cantril's analysis, although it is
not said outright, that those who participate in a social movement are
irrational and lack critical ability. Cantril does not entertain the possibility that it may in fact be the reverse—that those who join social
movements do so out of their critical abilities to analyze the social context, and those who do not are simply relying on the interpretations or
frame of reference of the hegemonic class.

The Second Period of the Sociology of Social Movements

The second period runs approximately from the late 1950s to the early 1970s. Neil Smelser's *Theory of Collective Behavior* can be seen as a bridge between the first and second periods of social movement sociology (Garner, 1997) and is a good example of second-period sociology. Because later theorists of the second period begin developing many of the forms of analysis that we see in the current sociology of social movements, I will look only at Smelser's work in this section before proceeding to an analysis of current work.

Neil Smelser

In *Theory of Collective Behavior*, Smelser (1962) sets out to address "the sad state of available research" (p. 3) on collective behavior by applying the rigorous standards of empirical-based social science to a phenomenon that had largely been studied by "speculative thinkers." Smelser begins by defining the domain of the term *collective behavior*. For Smelser, collective behavior includes the panic response, the craze response, hostile outbursts, norm-oriented movements, and value-oriented movements. In defining collective behavior, Smelser distinguishes himself from Brown (1954) and Blumer (1957) by focusing on the spread of belief instead of on the physical size of the collective or on temporal cohesiveness, as does Brown, or on forms of communication or interaction, as does Blumer. For Smelser (1962), collective behavior is "mobilization on the basis of a belief which redefines social action" (p. 8). It is important to note that Smelser also distinguishes himself from social psychological perspectives that consider participants in collective behavior as irrational (p. 11).

Smelser identifies six determinants of collective behavior, using what he calls a *value-added approach*. Determinants combined in a definite pattern, with each additional determinant increasingly narrowing possible behaviors, must be present for collective behavior to occur. The six determinants are structural conduciveness, structural strain, growth and spread of a generalized belief, precipitating factors, mobilization of participants, and social control. Smelser's focus, however, is on structural strain and generalized beliefs.

Smelser argues that collective behavior can be studied using the same analytical framework that one uses to study all social behavior. Having stated this, he then outlines the components of social action using the functionalist perspective developed by Talcott Parsons. He lays out the four components of social action (values, norms, mobilization of motivation into organized action, and situational facilities) and the seven levels of specificity that the components share. Smelser's analysis culminates in a value-added graph, with the four components on the horizontal axis and the levels of specificity on the vertical axis. Moving to the right or downward increases the specificity of the social action.

Collective behavior, for Smelser is the result of structural strain defined as "impairment of the relations among and consequently inadequate functioning of the components of action" (p. 47). Structural strain usually occurs at the lower, more specific levels of any of the four components of action. Placed within the Parsonian framework of social action, collective behavior, then, is more specifically defined as "an uninstitutionalized mobilization for action in order to modify one or more kinds of strain on the basis of a generalized reconstitution of a component of action" (p. 71). In other words, when strain arises at a given level of a component of action, people reconstitute a higher level of that component and, based on the more generalized belief of the higher level, act directly on the strain at the lower, more specific, level.

One can become quickly captivated by the tidiness and seemingly all-encompassing nature of Smelser's four-component, seven-level graph of social action and the ease with which he can locate therein any form of collective behavior. Drawing so heavily from Parsons, however, Smelser's analysis ultimately falls victim to the limits of functionalism. His graph of social action, the foundation of his analysis of collective behavior, is ahistorical in its attempt to be transhistorical and is therefore incapable of accounting for revolutionary transformation in which whole new societies are created. Within his framework, social change of any kind merely ripples on the surface of a society that is never qualitatively transformed. Furthermore, his focus on beliefs and his notion that "values are the major premises of the social order" (p. 35) fail to ground ideas, beliefs, and values (consciousness) in a dialectical relationship to the mode of production of a given society, and this leaves consciousness floating in the air. We see this most clearly in his placement of revolutions in the category of value-oriented movements along with messianic movements, sect formation, and charismatic movements, among others. In his analysis of value-oriented movements, Smelser fails to place the origins of revolutionary values or movements in the historical development of a given society. He points to the six determinants of social action, but the values seem to be ever present. Revolutionary movements and revolutionary ideas emerge as a result of the continuous changing nature of material life. Marx's classic analysis shows how revolutions have consistently occurred at the point at which the relations of production become fetters on the further development of the forces of production.

We can see, then, that the early work on collective behavior was steeped in a very functionalist, psychologistic, and individualist perspective. U.S. society at the time, at least in the minds of these sociologists, was seen as harmonious and able to meet the needs of its members.

Therefore, any collective action was seen as outside "conventional" or "normal" behavior. The social movements that emerged in the 1960s, however, shattered these perspectives by exposing several inadequacies in their ability to describe and explain these movements. The mass-society perspective was challenged by the fact that social movements emerged in societies such as the United States and Europe, which are democracies characterized by "civil societies with a multiplicity of voluntary associations" (Cohen, 1985, p. 672). The activists of the 1960s student movement were not deviant or economically deprived and therefore did not fit the ideal type of the collective behavior participant. These were largely middle-class youth from stable backgrounds (Habermas, 1970). Furthermore, many of the movements were not responses to economic breakdown but were pursuing concrete political goals with concrete tactics appropriate for the situations at hand (Cohen, 1985, p. 673; Zald, 1992, p. 331). Finally, with these movements, collective action became a part of political action and not separate from it, as previously theorized (Zald, 1992, p. 331). In short, the social movement theorists of the 1960s could not explain the social movements erupting around them; this led to a reevaluation of the theory and the development of the two major social movement theory approaches of today.

The Third Period of the Sociology of Social Movements

Current sociological thinking on social movements is dominated by two approaches: resource mobilization theory and new social movement theory. Fundamentally, resource mobilization theory attempts to understand how social movements mobilize, and new social movement theory attempts to understand why social movements arise (Foweraker, 1995, p. 2; Melucci, 1984, p. 821). Although this rather simplistic dichotomization overshadows subtle differences in the two major approaches, it does provide a good starting point from which to explore each approach more profoundly.

Resource Mobilization Theory

Resource mobilization theory (RM) emerged in the United States in the early 1970s and is now the dominant approach in this country. Mueller (1992) states that in the 1970s, 56 percent of articles on social movements in four of the field's major publications used RM, and by the early 1980s this was up to nearly 75 percent (p. 3). RM was a response to the inadequacies of earlier theory; this is evidenced by two of RM's central assumptions, which run counter to collective behavior assumptions: "(1) social movement activities are not spontaneous and disorganized and (2) social movement participants are not irrational" (Ferree, 1992, p. 29).

Klandermans (1991) provides a summary of RM in which he identifies three key elements. First, "the *cost and benefits of participation* [italics added] play an important role in the analysis of mobilization processes" (p. 24). Here researchers attempt to understand why rational individuals do not participate in collective action when the goals are in their interest, and, conversely, why individuals do participate when there seems to be no clear incentive. Second, "according to the resource mobilization approach, *organization* [italics added] is an important resource for a social movement" (p. 25). Organization is important in lowering the cost of participation, in the recruitment of new participants, and in increasing the chance of goal achievement. Third, *"expectations of success* [italics added] play an important role with respect to the collective incentives of participation" (p. 26). In other words, participation in the social movement increases if victory seems to be in reach or at least possible.

New Social Movement Theory

New social movement (NSM) theory emerged primarily in Western Europe in the 1970s and has grown to be the dominant approach in Europe and increasingly important in the United States. The newness of NSMs stems largely from the dwindling strength of trade unions and working-class parties (old social movements) and the emergence of the peace, environmental, women's, and identity movements in Europe and the United States. That these new movements actually exhibit "new" characteristics is debated (D'Anieri, Ernst, & Kier, 1990; Kivisto, 1986; Plotke, 1990; Tucker, 1991), yet for the most part it is accepted as true. In Western Europe the trade unions and working-class political parties have historically been much stronger and more important politically than in the United States, and, therefore, as they were overshadowed by NSMs, European theorists began to reassess their understanding of social movements. According to Foweraker (1995), because these "old" social movements (OSMs) have not been as significant in the United States, NSM theory did not take hold here early in its development. NSM theory, however, has increased in popularity in the United States along with its theoretical partner, postindustrial society analysis. Specifically, NSM theorists argue that the OSMs corresponded to industrial society and that with a new post-industrial society come NSMs, although some would argue that this is not what gives NSMs their newness (Cohen, 1985, pp. 664–665).

Klandermans (1991) sees agreement on three characteristics that theorists claim distinguish NSMs from OSMs. First, in terms of values, "new social movements do not accept the premises of a society based on economic growth" (p. 26). Second, "new social movements make extensive use of unconventional forms of action" (p. 27). Third, NSMs draw on a different constituency than OSMs. The two populations that are most likely to join NSMs are those "who have been marginalized by societal development" associated with modernization, and those of the middle classes who "have become particularly sensitive to problems resulting from modernization" (p. 27).

It should be noted that while these two approaches are distinct, Cohen (1985) shows that they do have commonalities. "Both paradigms assume that social movements involve contestation between organized groups with autonomous associations and sophisticated forms of communication.... Both argue that conflictual collective action is normal.... Both approaches distinguish between two levels of collective action: ... large scale mobilizations ... and the less visible, latent level of forms of organization and communication among groups" (p. 673). These shared assumptions move Cohen to suggest that each theory can inform the other. This sentiment is shared by Neidhardt and Rucht (1991), who "argue, along with other authors, for a closer linkage of the 'New Social Movements Approach' and the 'Resource Mobilization Approach' " (p. 443).

THE POLITICS OF SOCIAL MOVEMENTS

Having given the context of the development of social movement theory within sociology, I will now turn to an analysis of the major positions on what I call the politics of social movements. As stated earlier, it should be understood that the *politics of social movements* refers to the perceived potential of social movements to be agents of significant social change. The literature addressing this theme can be broken down into two broad categories that are largely based on people's position on the continued or diminished relevance of Marxism and, relatedly, their view of the nature of capitalist democracy today in light of postmodernism and globalization. The first category I call a *radical pluralist* position. These theorists are post-Marxists (Laclau & Mouffe, 1987) who reject major tenets of Marxist thought such as (a) the working class as the privileged agent of change, (b) the view that bourgeois democracy is hopelessly undemocratic, and (c) the belief that a revolution is necessary, possible, and a step forward for humanity. Using elements of postmodernist thought, these theorists reject grand theory, such as Marxism, and argue for "self-limiting" struggles for democratizing civil society. Furthermore, since these theorists see the notion of the working class as a privileged agent for change as a dead dream of an earlier modern epoch, they look to NSMs as best situated to democratize postmodern civil society.

The second category I call a *socialist* position; as we shall see, there are three major tendencies within this broad position. As a whole, however, these theorists are primarily neo-Marxists (one sees almost no classical Marxism in the academic literature). By and large, neo-Marxists reject

Marxism-Leninism but not the ultimate goal of socialism. They continue to see the working class as important for social change but feel that Marxism must be revised in theory and practice to incorporate social movements either as equal partners located within the working class or as potential allies socially situated in the middle class. Within the broad category of what I call socialist thinkers on social movements is a minority view that is quite skeptical of the potential of social movements to promote fundamental, lasting social change. These theorists argue that social movements tend to be temporary, heterogeneous, and easily co-opted by the state and are therefore incapable of sustaining the long-term struggle necessary for fundamental social change.

Beginning with the radical pluralist position, I will now turn to a more profound analysis of the various tendencies within these two broad categories.

The Radical Pluralists

The thought of Italian sociologist Alberto Melucci (1981, 1984, 1989, 1992) exemplifies the radical pluralist position on the importance of social movements in a postindustrial society. He argues that "we need a self-limiting concept of emancipation, mindful of the dark side of the modern myths, like progress, liberation and revolution" (1992, p. 73). A revolution against the state is not necessary because "as a unitary agent of intervention and action, the state has dissolved" (p. 70). For Melucci, "social movements can prevent the system from closing in upon itself by obligating the ruling groups to innovate, to permit change among elites" (p. 73).

Cohen (1985) echoes many of Melucci's radical pluralist positions in discussing the "newness" of NSMs. She argues that unique to NSMs "is a self-understanding that abandons revolutionary dreams in favor of the idea of structural reform, along with a defense of civil society that does not seek to abolish the autonomous functioning of political and economic systems—in a phrase, self-limiting radicalism" (p. 664). So for Cohen, like Melucci, NSMs limit themselves to protecting autonomy and identity within civil society and do not attack or attempt to take over the state or economy because revolution is a myth or a dream.

Touraine (1985), one of the foremost European theorists on social movements, also falls within the radical pluralist category. In contrasting social movements with revolutionary (socialist) activity, Touraine says, "The novelty of the concept of social movement . . . is that it opposes itself to this type of social thought and emphasizes the analytical separation between social movements and transformations of the State" (p. 775). Further clarifying the distinction between social movements and socialism, Touraine declares, "The idea of social movement is clearly anti-Leninist and implies that the nature of a social movement can be defined only in terms of cultural stakes and conflicts between social, 'civil' actors" (p. 776).

As may be apparent, the position of the radical pluralists in many ways is rooted in the work of Jürgen Habermas, who has also dedicated some of his work to discussing the relationship of NSMs to his theory of communicative action. Habermas (1984) argues that steering crises in modern capitalist society are overcome through what he calls a further "colonization of the lifeworld" (p. 299). This colonization, in part, takes the form of "the consumerist redefinition of private life spheres and personal life styles" (Habermas, 1981, p. 36). He claims that OSMs were offensive, and apart from the feminist movement, which follows the old idea of "universalist foundations of morality and legality . . . of an offensive movement" (p. 34), NSMs are defensive. The defensive, or resistance and withdrawal, movements "aim at stemming formally organized domains of action for the sake of communicatively structured domains, and not at conquering new territory" (p. 307). NSMs are key to Habermas's theory of communicative action because "it is possible to conceive of these conflicts [new social movements] in terms of resistance to tendencies toward colonization of the lifeworld" (p. 307).

Carl Boggs (1976, 1983, 1984, 1986) is exemplary of a current among radical pluralists who were socialists and have slowly transformed into postmodernists. Ellen Meiksins Wood (1998c) describes this process as the "retreat from class." In looking back over the trajectory of this tendency on the left, Wood says "that post-Marxism was just a short pitstop on the way to *anti*-Marxism" (p. xii). Boggs is more troublesome in that not only does he take the road from socialism to accommodation with anti-Marxism in academia, but he tries to bring Gramsci along with him. Although I have dealt with the distortions of Gramsci by radical pluralists and social democrats elsewhere (Holst, 1999), it is useful to briefly trace Boggs's evolution because it is typical of former socialists in academia who have fallen sway to postmodernism.

In *Gramsci's Marxism*, Boggs (1976) provides one of the earliest book-length treatments of Gramsci's Marxism in English. In this work, Boggs makes clear the affinities of Gramsci and Lenin. By 1983, however, Boggs has begun his journey to anti-Marxism by attacking fellow academics who continue to work within a Marxist framework. Boggs (1984) then reworks his earlier version of Gramsci. "Whereas my earlier book stressed the basic thematic unity and continuity in Gramsci—organized largely around a picture of him as a 'democratic' variant of Lenin—*The Two Revolutions* emphasizes a . . . changing Gramsci" (p. viii). His further clarification of his new approach to Gramsci is revealing because we see the building of the theoretical justification of social movement politics over class politics through the use of Gramsci that is prominent in

Boggs's later work. "To the extent that the Gramsci who emerged from *Gramsci's Marxism* was a Lenin . . . in the context of Italy, . . . I understood this as a positive new synthesis. In *The Two Revolutions*, on the other hand, the Leninist . . . side of Gramsci is viewed quite differently: it is defined as a residue . . . which tends to *block* those democratic and culturally subversive tendencies" (p. ix). Boggs (1986), who subsequently abandons a working-class–based socialist struggle that he says "appears to have exhausted its potential" (p. 248), now must go back and cover his own Leninist tracks, along with those of Gramsci that he showed us in 1976. Obviously, one must be granted the continuing right to reassess one's earlier work, but the problem that Boggs so exquisitely exemplifies is what can only be called distortions of Gramsci for contemporary political contexts. From Boggs's revision of Gramsci we get statements such as the following: (a) "It is now possible to see more clearly what Gramsci apparently did not see at all" (p. ix); (b) "I have taken the liberty of establishing certain linkages . . . even though such linkages are nowhere explicitly made in the *Notebooks*" (p. xi); and (c) "I have further used the concepts 'prefigurative' and 'counter-hegemonic' . . . despite the fact that Gramsci himself never adopted such terms" (p. xi). Therefore, with Boggs's reworking of Gramsci we are left with a text that he himself says "many will probably find . . . unrecognizable as an extension of [the earlier] study" (p. xii).

As we see in Boggs's later (1986) work, the democratic and cultural tendencies he now emphasizes in Gramsci are references to modern-day social movements. Thus, when Boggs is a Leninist fellow traveler, so is Gramsci, but when Boggs changes political stripes, he decides to put new ones on Gramsci as well. Once he has abandoned class and a working-class–based socialist politic in accord with the Marxist tradition, it becomes essential to develop a new political ideology: post-Marxism.

In *Social Movements and Political Power*, Boggs (1986) identifies the following ten points of departure for what he calls the post-Marxist position on NSMs:

1. The historical clash between Marxism and NSMs leads not to the reconstruction of Marxism as a unified theory but instead to its insoluble crisis and ultimately to its transcendence.

2. The very appearance of the new movements refutes the Marxist notion that the working class is the revolutionary agent to overthrow capitalism.

3. The heterogeneity of the various movements shows that there is no one privileged agent.

4. The expanding bureaucracy of the state has spawned new forms of resistance evident in NSMs.

5. The form of resistance of NSMs is fundamentally different from that of OSMs.

6. NSMs resist integration into the state or the political system.

7. Feminism offers alternative forms of organization and leadership diametrically opposed to that of OSMs.

8. Ecological problems expose the bankruptcy of both capitalist and socialist modernization projects.

9. The peace movement cannot be explained with Marxist class analysis.

10. NSMs stress quality of life and cultural issues not addressed by merely putting the control of production into the hands of workers.

The Socialists

Whereas the radical pluralists see NSMs as signaling the death of Marxism, the socialists see them as offering an opportunity to review and revise Marxism without giving up the ultimate goal of socialism. They do not advocate "self-limiting" struggle, but a struggle that is merely taking on different forms with emerging actors (NSMs). Among the socialists there is a three-sided debate that revolves around an analysis of the social location of NSMs and, therefore, the relationship of these movements to the working class. The socialists can accept the radical pluralist argument of a new historical actor (NSMs), but the issue is whether this marks a qualitative rupture in the development of capitalism. For the radical pluralists, clearly the answer is affirmative. NSMs mark the beginning of the postmodern and/or postindustrial epoch and the end of modernity and industrial capitalism; therefore, we must say "farewell to the working class" (Gorz, 1982) and the goal of socialism. The socialists, on the other hand, do not view NSMs as a manifestation of a qualitative transformation to a postindustrial or postmodern capitalism. The three major positions among socialists are as follows: (a) NSMs are important agents of change that have emerged alongside a changing working class and peasantry (where present) that must be forged into some form of coalition to effect fundamental social change; (b) NSM issues and actors are working class, and we must adjust our analysis of late capitalist class structure to include those social sectors active in NSMs within our definition of who constitutes the working class; and (c) NSMs are largely middle-class movements that are temporary, easily co-opted by bourgeois democracy, and therefore largely ineffective for fundamental social transformation. They are symptomatic more of the left's weakness and backwardness than its strength and connectedness with the masses of working people (Navarro, 1991, p. 55).

Socialists Advocating an OSM-NSM Coalition Politics

Writing from Nicaragua, Núñez Soto (1989) argues that "people have ceased to believe in liberal institutions and have rejected socialist reductionism [economistic Marxism-Leninism], which does not mean that they reject democracy or socialism, as some thinkers like to think" (p. 10). Furthermore, he says that "the social movements are militantly popular. . . . they are in no sense a negation of revolution" (p. 10). Burbach and Núñez (1987) articulate the notion of a third force for socialism alongside workers and peasants, who, they argue, are the fundamental forces. This third force "comprise[s] a number of diverse social groups and social movements that are defined more by their social and political attributes than by their relationship to the work-place" (p. 64). However, they argue, "the origin of their exploitation is in the evolution of capitalist society as a whole" (p. 64), and they "need to be won over for the triumph of the political revolution; their continued support and involvement are also necessary for the social revolution to begin to build a classless socialist society" (p. 65).

More recently, Burbach (1998) has taken this analysis in a post-Marxist direction, although, unlike most post-Marxists, he remains committed to socialism. In terms of a critique of Marxism, Burbach's post-Marxism parallels that of Boggs outlined above. Unlike Boggs, however, Burbach is interested in the political potential of what he calls the *castaways*. "We have to look to the large and growing sector of humanity that has been variously called the underclass, the marginalized, or the castaways of the capitalist world" (p. 59). Interestingly, this is the same sector that Gorz (1982) looked to nearly twenty years ago and the same sector that the orthodox Marxist Communist Labor Party (1991), now the League of Revolutionaries for a New America (1998), sees as the most revolutionary segment of the working class. According to Burbach (1998), "in the parts of the world that capitalism discards, forms of production are taking hold that comprise what could be called postmodern economies. . . . The most extensive of the postmodern economies consists of the informal sector: the ever more numerous street vendors, the flea markets, petty family businesses, and even garbage scavengers" (p. 60). Within the postmodern economies, he also includes laid-off workers from the corporate sector who set up small cottage enterprises to subcontract. All of these segments of postmodern economies form a mode of production that "are not a part of the existent system" (p. 61). Burbach says that this emergent mode of production represents associate producers and the creation of socialism alongside the capitalist mode of production. These sectors can be linked with NSMs, whose representatives "have the potential to understand and articulate what is going on among the ever swelling numbers of castaways" (p. 62).

The themes of the rejection of Marxism-Leninism but not socialism and of the need to form an alliance between the working class and NSMs are also present in the work of Carroll and Ratner (1994) and Epstein (1990). Carroll and Ratner (1994) argue that "the rigidities of Leninist views on socialist politics may have consigned orthodox Marxism to the status of historical relic, but equally problematic is the radical pluralist disavowal of any materialist-grounded, unifying basis for counter-hegemony" (p. 3). They, like other socialists, believe that Gramsci offers an alternative socialist theory and practice to Leninism. Important to Carroll and Ratner is what they see as Gramsci's notion of building counter-hegemony within civil society. They define civil society as "a realm of activity distinct from the state and capitalist production in which many aspects of social and political identity (such as gender and ethnicity) are fundamentally grounded" (p. 6). Here, of course, they are referring to the actions of NSMs. They see NSMs as part of the counter-hegemonic politics necessary for socialism because many of the activities of NSMs constitute resistance to the power of capital, and therefore "there is a strong basis in their practice for counter-hegemonic coalition formation" (p. 18) between the working class and NSMs.

In a very similar vein, Epstein (1990) says, "Gramsci argued that the creation of a hegemonic project involves the construction of an historic bloc" (p. 60). In articulating exactly who are the agents poised to create this historic bloc, Epstein looks to the working class, or the bottom third of society, and the middle third of society, or those middle-class people who form the majority of those active in NSMs. "One of the most difficult tasks of the left in the nineties and beyond will be constructing a 'progressive' alliance, persuading the middle third to identify its interests with the lower third in the context of declining resources, and persuading the bottom third that economic growth is not the answer" (p. 62).

NSMs as Part of the Working Class

Wilde (1990) and Navarro (1988) also see the possibility of workers and NSMs working together, but not in a coalition. A coalition is not necessary because the NSMs are part of the working class, in their view. Wilde (1990) argues that it is possible "to adhere to marxian class analysis and at the same time enthuse over the emancipatory potential of new social movements" (p. 55). He looks to neo-Marxist writers such as Erik Olin Wright (1979, 1985) who attempt to revise Marxist class analysis to include workers in the white-collar service sector. This is the sector from which participants in NSMs usually come, and they have commonly been seen by Marxists as not having a material interest in socialism. Drawing from Wright, however, Wilde argues that material interest goes beyond economic standard of living to include NSM issues of quality of life, peace, a clean environment, and so forth. Therefore, Wilde (1990) says, "the concerns being voiced by new social movements *are* material, and the issues addressed are products of the class structure of the world capitalist system" (p. 66). He goes on to add, "New social movements also contain a potential for the development of class consciousness. They are not, as most theorists would claim, non-class movements, or even cross-class movements; they are protest movements *within* [italics added] the working class whose attentions are not primarily on the work place but on society as a whole" (pp. 66–67).

Philion (1998), specifically addressing the environmental movement, argues that this particular NSM raises issues of class. "Social movements that arise in response to these unintended consequences of 'growth' policies [health and ecological problems] are intrinsically challenging capital's capacity to be flexible. No less than traditional trade union–based movements, they are challenging capital and are therefore, theoretically speaking, quite capable of possessing a subjectivity within the framework of classical Marxist class analysis" (p. 89). Furthermore, he adds, when NSMs do not articulate their issues—which *are* concerns of the working class—in terms of class, they are by and large ineffectual. "The present state of social movements, especially in the United States, *as they are presently geared toward middle-class constituencies,* is a considerably weak and ineffective one.... Two of the most prominent new social movements, namely, the feminist ... and environmental movements ..., have suffered from their inability or even unwillingness to articulate their movements' goals in ways that could potentially win over larger numbers of the disenfranchised working class" (p. 91).

Shukra (1997), also writing about a particular NSM—Black Power in England—argues that what she sees as the artificial separation between the NSM of Black Power and the trade union movement was the result of an erroneous historical choice made by left activists who opted for a narrow separatist or identity politic instead of challenging the trade union movement to widen its focus to include the question of racism that affects working-class minorities.

Faced with the development of post-1968 social movements, the different fractions of the left were confronted with the problem of linking them to the trade union movement and somehow metamorphosising them all into a coherent movement for change.... However, the "new social movements" produced alternative spontaneities which allowed them, and the left, to avoid changing existing forms of limited consciousness.... Rather than consider how a wider working-class consciousness might be shaped, ... much of the left ... appears to have conflated the two forms of consciousness. In doing so, a key for liberatory consciousness was lost; that by definition, the working class needed to produce a politics of anti-oppression as well as anti-exploitation as a prerequisite to developing a working-class consciousness which would be a key to destroying all forms of oppression through revolutionary social change. (pp. 235–236)

The question of the relationship between class consciousness, NSMs, and peasants is raised by Brass (1991), who also insists that the issues of NSMs are issues of the working class and peasantry. Because Marxism has not adequately studied the development of class consciousness, this leaves the door open for radical pluralists to claim that the demands and ideas of NSMs mark a new epoch in capitalism.

New social movement theory argue[s] that, as . . . mobilization and resistance to colonialism/capitalism has more to do with the experience and ideology of gender, ethnicity, region, ecology, or religion, these kinds of "difference" cannot be understood by (and are therefore not reducible to) the class position of the subject. This incompatibility between ethnic/gender/religious/regional identity and experience on the one hand, and class-specific ideological forms on the other, leads in turn and inevitably to the non-emergence of class consciousness, which is then taken as evidence for the non-existence of class itself. (p. 180)

In the debate over the newness of NSMs, the charge that NSMs are actually not very new is generally framed in class terms, centering on a continuity between OSMs and NSMs. One view (D'Anieri et al., 1990; Tucker, 1991) argues that NSM theorists fail to realize that, while many OSMs organized around economic issues, "many of the supposedly new characteristics can be found in past movements in a variety of historical epochs and geographical settings" (D'Anieri et al., 1990, p. 445). Tucker (1991) critiques the analysis of Cohen and Habermas through a study of nineteenth-century French syndicalism and concludes, "Syndicalism shares many of the same concerns with modern movements, ranging from the value of autonomy to an emphasis on rational (rather than traditional) modes of justification and consensus formation; further, the movement attempted to implement these values in its very organizational structure" (p. 86). Fundamentally, the problem with NSM theorists is that in their rush to declare a qualitative change in capitalism from industrialism to postindustrialism through largely structural analyses, they fail to see the specific historical and political contexts in which many OSMs operated (D'Anieri et al., 1990, p. 445). Conversely, a second view argues that the continuity runs the other way; NSMs are similar to OSMs in theme and target. For example, Adam (1993) states, "Though not centrally economic movements, the new social movements *do* address political economy. . . . While ambivalent about state power, the new social movements *do* address the state and are profoundly shaped by its actions. . . . The state is a primary and unavoidable agent in the reproduction of relations of domination in race, gender, sexuality, and environment and the new social movements struggle actively to block and re-make these mechanisms of subordination" (pp. 326–327). Furthermore, the concept of "newness" in terms of third-world social movements is not always relevant. "Social movements in the South are not by any means post-modern. . . . Whatever the relevance of characterizing Northern societies as post-industrial and post-modern, Southern societies for sure are not" (Schuurman, 1993, p. 191; see Slater, 1991, for a counterargument).

In addition, Wainwright (1995) reminds us that OSMs and NSMs are intrinsically linked by the sheer virtue of the overlap in activists and the mutual influence that these movements have on each other, particularly in the European context. "In Britain a complex lattice work of connections has grown up in which feminists, eco-, peace or anti-racist activists, for example, have had considerable influence on both the policies and ways of organizing of the trade unions and vice versa" (pp. 80–81). Adam (1993) agrees with this and raises the important and ironic fact that many socialists are "born" out of the struggles of NSMs and thereby infuse them with a praxis of "a comprehensive worldview which recognizes and supports subordinated people wherever they exist" (p. 330).

Finally, also within the socialist perspective of NSMs is the work of Fuentes and Frank (1989, 1990). Their perspective is somewhat unique because they operate within the world systems analysis developed by Immanuel Wallerstein. It is interesting to note that they turn the new versus old social movements debate on its head by arguing that OSMs such as trade unions are relatively new, and NSMs such as the women's movement date back centuries (Fuentes & Frank, 1989, pp. 179–180). Furthermore, they see the importance of NSMs in civil society but make no reference to Gramsci or a historical bloc. They point to the perceived weaknesses of social movements and then state that "it may be asked how social movements can be cyclical, temporary, defensive, mutually conflicting and weak . . . and at the same time forge new links that serve to transform society." They say that "the answer may be . . . found in the participation and contribution by social movements to extending and redefining democracy in civil society" (p. 190). They believe that civil society is increasingly important as the state becomes less and less significant with globalization. Social movements in civil society, therefore, become key players as they "shift the socio-political center of gravity from institutional political or economic democracy . . . in the state toward more participatory civil democracy and power in civil society and culture" (p. 191).

The Socialist Skeptics

One of the most articulate advocates of the socialist skeptic view is sociologist Michael Burawoy (1989). He argues that "new social movements, while making significant advances within the confines of liberal democracy, do not move us beyond capitalism" (p. 61). In fact, he says "capitalism deflects struggles away from itself and toward the expansion of democracy. By virtue of capital's mobility, capitalism contains those struggles within bounds of its own production" (p. 73). He further argues that reform struggles for greater democracy are not only reflected by capitalism but also "renew the dynamism of capitalism" (p. 72). The problem of NSMs being deflected from challenging the heart of capitalist power is also reflected in the ideas of Calderon and Santos (1987). "Social movements never confront the real opponents. In reality, they stay subjected to a defensive and resistant practice and with this reaction are only able to scrape the surface of a logic of power that is ever more abstract and diffuse while their resistance is ever more concrete and localized" (p. 193; my translation).

Kothari (1993) also cautions us about the transformative potential of NSMs. He says that "these movements have turned out to be major detractions from the basic struggles for power" and that "the fundamental challenge facing these movements is . . . wide-ranging cooptation by the system" (p. 133). Furthermore, he says, "the biggest failure of . . . new social movements lies in their inability to become part of a united political movement" (p. 134).

Ross (1995) puts his skepticism in the following terms:

The lingering tendency to compose a laundry list of various rebellious groups—the Left + social democrats + unionists + feminists + anti-racists + environmentalists + others—may work for demonstrations, but believing that all of these groups are "really" socialist is a dangerous illusion. Many are not socialist at all. The absence of unifying notions of progressivism plus the place of NSMs in parliamentary democratic systems establishes a situation in which most NSMs will seek out "pluralist" political deals from the establishment to benefit their own bases and causes. (p. 69)

Taylor (1997), like Ross, is wary of the lack of unity among NSMs. She sees the United Democratic Front (UDF) in South Africa as a unique example of NSMs leading to transformative community development. "If community development, as a process and strategy for social transformation which equalises power relations, is to succeed then those involved need to go beyond seeing new social movements as a panacea for people's struggles from below" (p. 263). For Taylor, NSMs are powerful to the extent that they converge with national popular interests and move beyond survival issues. In other words, NSMs were powerful in South Africa to the extent that they linked with the national liberation struggle through the UDF.

Finally, the problem of identity politics that divides rather than unifies, which I will take up in more detail in the concluding section of this chapter, is also a part of the skepticism that socialists have toward NSMs. This problem has been debated heavily within feminist circles, and Segal (1991) is exemplary of socialist-feminist critiques of identity-based feminism. She argues that "it is precisely the issues arising from what is most distinctively female that today most dramatically *divide* rather than unite feminists fighting for women's interests" (p. 87). This fracturing along the political line of identity, most visible in the United States, leads to a situation in which "despite the existence of the largest, most influential and vociferous feminist movement in the world, it is US women who have seen least *overall* change in the relative disadvantages of their sex, compared to other Western democracies" (p. 88). Considering the current political economic situation, she says that "at a time when the advances made by some women are so clearly overshadowed by the increasing poverty experienced so acutely by others (alongside the unemployment of men of their class and group) it seems perverse to pose women's specific interests *against* rather than *alongside* more traditional socialist goals" (p. 90). In the end, Segal argues, identity politics on its own "can offer little more than the enjoyment of an endless game of self-exploration played out on the great board of Identity" (p. 91).

CONCLUSION

At this point I would like to assess the literature on the politics of social movements covered thus far.

The Radical Pluralists

The Problems of Postmodernism

The radical pluralist perspective is riddled with flaws. Its acceptance of major tenets of postmodern thought is problematic. Drawing heavily on interpretations of the work of Michel Foucault and of Habermas, radical pluralists argue that characteristic of the postmodern condition is "local discursivities" (Foucault, 1980, p. 85) as opposed to a dominant capitalist political economy. Empirically, runs the argument, the emergence of many NSMs and the decline of the movement of labor against capital show that we have witnessed the end of modernity. Furthermore, since these movements are supposedly not interested in questions of political economy but seek autonomy for cultural or identity expression, we can speak of a pluralism of resistance based heavily on the politics of discourse. We can see many references to the "era" of discursivity, identity, and fragmentation in the literature on NSMs.

Referring to Habermas, Luke (1994) says that we can understand "new social movements as *fragmentary* efforts made by groups within an embattled but still existing civil society, struggling to defend their *independent identities and cultural autonomy* outside of the institutionalized structures of power and exchange in contemporary corporate capitalism [italics added]" (p. 243). The influence of Foucault is evident in the work of Brunt (1989) and, indeed, in the whole of the "New Times" political project of the British Communist Party, of which she is a member.

In order to work out political strategies that actually match the situations we're in, . . . we need a recognition that power is "omnipresent." . . . It is not simply, as it's previously been thought, a force coming from elsewhere, or above, or from a singly-directed source, and governed by one particular set of people, the ruling class. . . . [I]f power is everywhere, . . . then the political agenda is radically altered. It makes no sense to talk in any simple way of "the priorities" or "the main thing," against which other struggles are subordinated. (p. 157)

Both Slater (1991, 1994) and Escobar (1992) provide us with examples from Latin America. Escobar says that "what matters for a strategy of change is the formation of nuclei . . . or transformations around 'neuralgic knots' . . . through which a new *discursive* formation may slowly be articulated [italics added]" (p. 27). Slater (1991) adds that we "will have to start from broader and more heterogeneous bases than ever before. This also carries with it the clear implication that there are no *a priori* privileged points for politics" (p. 40).

The notion of discursivity is taken to its logical conclusion in what Epstein (1997, p. 136) calls "strong" postmodernism as evidenced by Brown (1994). "By declaring the 'death of the author,' structuralism has justly executed any notion of a subject prior to language. An essential identity will always elude us; and, learning from the postmodern 'incredulity towards metanarratives' . . . *we are limited to telling 'small stories from heterogeneous subject positions'* [italics added]" (p. 271).

The postmodernist view of NSMs as discursive and fragmented sites of resistance and identity formation is problematic on several fronts. First, a politics of discourse leads to the dead end of idealism. A politics of discourse that does not address the origins and continuing formation of language in social relations (McNally, 1997) and the dialectical relationship therein (Freire, 1984) wallows in the changing of language as political struggle. This most recent manifestation of idealism in postmodernism is part of the age-old struggle between idealism and materialism that Engels (1888/1959) identified more than 100 years ago and that continues today. This is most obvious in the "political correctness" debates over proper language usage that do not address the fundamental social relations at play. The third world remains "third" in terms of the continued asymmetrical international political economic relations whether we call it the "South" or the "developing world."

Second, as we have already seen, the very notion that NSMs are actually *new*—in other words, that they signal a qualitative change in the political economic arrangement of society and thereby also express qualitatively new forms of resistance—is dubious. Many of the NSMs are not

actually new (feminism, identity-nationalist movements, community autonomy movements). Furthermore, the targets of these movements are
still very often the state and the economy; most identity movements seek
civil rights through the state and equal protection in the economy. Autonomy movements are movements directed largely at state structures.
Additionally, Adam's (1993) understanding of the actual dynamics of
social movements is apparent to all who have sustained experience in
them. The NSMs are peppered with socialists, social democrats, Marxist-
Leninists, Maoists, Stalinists, Trotskyites, and so forth, all of whom are
supposedly of the OSMs. The left, particularly in the United States with
its historic lack of mass left-wing political parties, has a fluid mixture of
people, organizations, and aims of the OSMs and NSMs.

Third, the emphasis on the fragmentation of power and sites of resistance flies in the face of the political economic realities that form the very
basis of the emergence of such ideas—namely, the fall of self-proclaimed
communist states and the "triumph" of capitalism. The post–World War
II triumph of capital over labor, through compromises characterized as
labor's acquiescence to the dictates of capital at the point of production
for a greater share in the allocation of surplus value through wages or
social services, is generally seen by radical pluralists as one of the last
acts of OSMs. Frustration over the co-opted nature of the trade unions
and political parties that did not address the continued commodification
of life and the particular issues of marginalized groups led to the emergence of NSMs in the 1960s and 1970s. The events of 1989 mark the final
death of OSMs, which had already been moribund for more than four
decades. Post–World War II capitalism, however, has by no means been
a fragmented economic system. The fall of communism has demon-
strated this fact ever more clearly. The neoliberal model, George Bush's
"New World Order," is a unipolar world in which, according to Mar-
garet Thatcher, "There Is No Alternative." At a time when segments of
the left have abandoned ship for a politics of discourse and fragmentation, capitalism as a world economic system has become more universal
and unified, and therefore the socialist critique of it is increasingly relevant at the "end of history"; one only need review the commentaries
of Marx and Engels' "prophecies" in *The Communist Manifesto* in both
the left and mainstream presses in its 150th anniversary in 1998. This is
not to deny, however, the fact that the increasing universality of capitalism and the penetration of capitalist relations into "private" life do
bring an element of fragmentation and dislocation (Piven, 1995; Wood,
1998b, pp. 28–29), but it is precisely the source of this fragmentation in
capitalist relations that is obscured or denied in radical pluralist thought.
That is why they can claim that NSMs, in part anticapitalist in outlook
and that appeal to governments for action on their concerns, are non-

economic, discursive, and cultural movements that do not concern themselves with the state or economy.

Finally, as with discourse politics, the limits of identity politics are
clear.

The political struggle for gay and lesbian organizations pivots around the issue
of whether gays and lesbians can serve openly in the military, instead of on the
evils of militarism and the deaths of millions in U.S.-led wars. Black organizations fight for equality of opportunity in the FBI; Latino rights groups for inclusion in the Border Patrol and INS.... Identity politics sees individual
empowerment as the solution to victimization, but victimhood is not a sufficiently strong base on which to build a social justice movement, and empowerment is not a solution in a capitalist system whose everyday workings crush the
many in the interests of the few. (Anner, 1996, pp. 10–11)

Moreover, identity politics in its nationalist forms in communities of
color can also fall into the trap of neoliberalism. Community empowerment politics can play into the hands of government agencies eager to
privatize services in the name of community control and grassroots development. Let this not be interpreted, however, as a condemnation of
necessary nationalist struggles in situations of continued colonial and
national oppression.

The limits of identity politics have also been clearly seen in the
women's movement. Naiman (1996) describes the dilemma quite succinctly. "If . . . each category of oppression creates a different experiential
reality, if say, aboriginal women or working-class women or lesbians
each experience their 'women-ness' in a different way, what is it that can
bring them together?" (p. 14). The only way out of this ideological corner
is a return to discourse and the call for unity in diversity and celebrations
of difference. Yet, within all the talk of valuing others, the real needs for
social justice go unmet. As Ellen Meiksins Wood (1994) asks, "how could
one think of celebrating . . . class differences" (p. 28)? Indeed, here we see
the limits of radical pluralist thought excised of political economy. We
cannot celebrate class differences—the possession or nonpossession of
housing, levels of dietary sufficiency, and so forth. The radical pluralists
rarely address these issues because they do not have a "discourse" of
class. When they do address the question of capitalism and class, it is as
just one more form of oppression, with no privileged position. In the
end, this tells us more about the radical pluralist intellectuals than the
movements about which they write (Nugent, 1997).

Another problematic element in radical pluralist thought on NSMs is
the concept of a postindustrial society that forms part of the much
broader contemporary paradigm of globalization. Again, this argument

of radical pluralists is based on no political economy or a very questionable one.

Tabb (1997) has quite accurately broken down the arguments over globalization into the *strong* version and the *longer* version. The strong version, present in most radical pluralist discourse on social movements, argues that the working class, co-opted by the post–World War II welfare-state compromises in the 1950s and 1960s, all but disappeared by the 1980s in a postindustrial era. As the argument goes, a combination of automation and technology has reduced industrial production jobs and has also allowed them to be shifted to low-wage areas anywhere on the planet. The "new" economy is an information or postindustrial economy characterized by the global and instantaneous movement of unprecedented amounts of finance and information-based capital that makes the old nation-state economies, and therefore the nation-state itself, irrelevant; we are witnessing an economy with multinational corporations that operate on a truly global scale. Because we have no industry, we have no workers and, therefore, no working-class–based politics of OSMs. Furthermore, the state, unable to rein in global capital and further weakened by the very international mechanisms of global capital (the IMF, World Bank, etc.), is no longer a useful site for social change. Resistance is taken up by new non–working-class actors and is located in the social terrain between or outside the economy and state with the goal of protecting the private and intimate spheres of life, which are increasingly penetrated or "colonized" by the new information economy.

The longer version is based in classical Marxist political economy and, as the name would indicate, takes a historical view of the long development of capitalism in its assessment of contemporary capitalism. Fundamentally, the longer version, in contrast to the strong version, argues that we have not seen a qualitative change, or "rupture," in capitalist relations in production. As Mandel (1975) argued, we are still in the long wave of monopoly, or late capitalism, that Lenin (1917/1939) identified more than eighty years ago. Specifically, we can identify three areas of disagreement that those of the longer version raise in response to the strong version of globalization.

First, capitalism has always been global. "Globalization is not a condition or a phenomenon: it is a process that has been going on . . . ever since capitalism came in the world as a viable form of society four or five centuries ago" (Sweezy, 1997, p. 1). Indeed, it is precisely this fact that makes Marx's works *The Communist Manifesto* and *Capital* so contemporary. Globalization, we see today, is the restarting of mid- to late-nineteenth-century processes that were interrupted by two world wars, the Depression, and the opting out of the world capitalist system of the socialist camp and the subsequent Cold War that this initiated. That is why some have argued that the world economy was actually more glob-alized before World War I than today (Tabb, 1997, p. 24).

Second, the idea of the Fordist or welfare state compromise or co-optation of the working class in the post–World War II era ignores labor history, especially in the United States. The year 1946 witnessed the greatest wave of strikes in U.S. history (Milton, 1982, p. 154).

We have to keep in mind that the so-called golden age was a period when capital sustained its profits not by "accords" so much as by vicious class conflict: from Taft-Hartley in the late 1940s, to union-avoidance strategies . . . or deunionization strategies . . . in the late fifties and early sixties, to savage bouts of union-busting and "some of the worst storms in labor history" in the late fifties, followed by a decade of union unrest from the early sixties to the early seventies, with a rank-and-file chafing against their leadership's inadequate responses to attacks by cap-ital. (Wood, 1998a, p. 34)

In addition, on the international stage the struggle between capital and labor as embodied in imperialist relations has not seen a qualitative change; capital then and now has engaged in brutal attacks upon labor. "The difference between the so-called Keynesian period and today is that in earlier days there was a hush-hush aspect to the discipline imposed on the third world, whereas now neo-liberal principles are loudly pro-claimed as the true faith" (Magdoff, 1998, p. 7).

Third, we have not moved into a postindustrial economy in which production can be or is moved easily from the North to the South (hem-ispheres). Moody (1997) provides very convincing data in this regard. As he argues, the distribution of economic activity between the North and the South has not changed drastically in the last twenty-five years. The majority of production is still carried on in the North. "Much of the loss in jobs and income among workers in the North is not the direct result of export of capital or jobs, *per se*, but of a combination of neoli-beral policies and cost-cutting efforts within the North itself" (p. 53). Quoting UN statistics, he shows that the South's share of world manu-facturing output has changed from only 11.7 percent in 1975 to 15.4 per-cent in 1993 (p. 55). Moreover, in terms of foreign direct investment (FDI), an indicator of globalization by those of the strong version, 94–98 percent of it is controlled by the North and 80 percent of it is invested within the North itself (p. 56). Moody's evidence of the nature of man-ufacturing production and jobs in the North versus the South concurs with Keller's (1983) historical analysis of the political economic relation-ship between the northern part of the United States and what he consid-ers to be the colonized southern nation (i.e., the southeastern Black Belt area). "Late in an economic period the industries which are in crisis begin to be transplanted to the South as the North modernizes its economic base.... Rather than abandoning less profitable industries altogether their profitability can be stretched out by shifting them southward to take advantage of the cheaper national labor market. At the same time new, more technically advanced industries can be built up in the North" (p. 83). In looking back on the decade of the 1990s, Moody concludes that "the notion of a single seamless world economy was still far from a reality in the mid-1990s. What was real, however, was the universalizing of capitalism: operating both nationally in more places and internationally at various levels" (p. 42).

Of greatest importance are the political implications that can be drawn from the contrasts between the strong and longer versions of globalization. As we have already seen, the strong version is the political economy of radical pluralist NSM politics. In turn, the longer version is the political economy of a distinct politic that does not abandon socialism or the working class. There are two major political implications for a longer version of globalization. First, the working class is still a privileged agent for fundamental social change. As NSMs have waned, exposing the limits of identity politics, the working class has put itself back in the forefront of the struggle against neoliberalism in the North and the South.

The mass political strikes that hit Nigeria, Indonesia, Taiwan, France, South Korea, Italy, Belgium, Canada, South Africa, Brazil, Argentina, Paraguay, Panama, Bolivia, Greece, Spain, Venezuela, Haiti, Columbia, Ecuador, and elsewhere from 1994 on into 1997 were not called by political parties, as they often had been in past decades. Rather they were meant to fill a political vacuum created by the retreats of the old parties of the left. It was the working class itself, led or at least accompanied by its unions, that was taking on the right-wing/neoliberal (conservative) agenda.... These political strikes were mainly in the public sector. ... Bitter strikes in North America, Britain, Germany and elsewhere were waged around issues associated with new methods of work organization. (Moody, 1997, p. 10)

The aim of these strikes is to stop the implementation of neoliberal policies. This fact highlights the second major implication of the longer version of globalization: the increasing importance of the state as both a target for working-class opposition and an instrument for capital's drive to impose neoliberal policies. It must be kept in mind that what we see as globalization or neoliberal policies are precisely *policies*—in other words, specific political choices (not inevitabilities) made by those with the power to use the nation-state as an instrument to maintain or enhance profitability. Contrary to the prognostications of the "end of the nation-state" under globalization (see, e.g., Guéhenno, 1995), "in the global market, capital *needs* the state. It needs the state to maintain the conditions of accumulation, to preserve labor discipline, to enhance the mobility of capital while suppressing the mobility of labor. . . . If anything, the nation-state is the *main agent* of globalization" (Wood, 1997, p. 12). Therefore, as Wood argues, globalization has made "class politics—a politics directed at the state, and at class power concentrated in the state—more rather than less important, more rather than less possible" (p. 8). This particular class politic is about the class character of the state and not welfare-state reforms. In the last twenty years, with all the talk of the end of history, the bankruptcy of socialism, the end of the working class, and so on, what we have really seen is the polarization of wealth, "society as a whole . . . more and more splitting up into two great hostile camps" (Marx & Engels, 1848/1948, p. 9) and the end of social democracy as an option.

I would like to focus on one final aspect of radical pluralist thought that I find problematic. Although Wood (1997) highlights the inadequate treatment of the renewed importance of the state in fostering neoliberalism in radical pluralist thought, another aspect of this question is the role of the state as an instrument of repression. For all their talk of NSMs coming to the "defense of the lifeworld" and civil society, very little mention is made of the role of the state in repressing these efforts even when they are not interested in seizing state power. As Jenkins (1995) says, "the relationship between the state and social movements constitutes a major gap in the existing literature. . . . Social movement scholars have primarily focused on those who are contesting power rather than their relationships with the powerful" (p. 15). While we can agree that neoliberal privatization in the North and structural adjustment programs in the South have scaled back the social service sector of the state, there is little or no evidence that the repressive apparatus (army, police, judicial system) is disappearing. These elements of the state have historically been used to crush social movements and therefore cannot be ignored. Moreover, it is not enough to simply state that social movements avoid this problem because of their desire to build or protect civil society instead of seizing state power. On the one hand, a nonstatist strategy does not protect social movements from state repression; one need only remember the equally brutal repression of the Republic of New Africa and the Black Panther Party when the former openly declared its opposition to the revolutionary politics of the latter (Obadele, 1972). On the other hand, the whole concept of building or protecting civil society is problematic. This is the topic of the next chapter, so suffice it to say at this point that the notion of an autonomous civil society ripe for democratization is very vague. The idea that there is actually a civil society relatively free of the state and the market flies in the face of nearly all progressive social theory, from Marx and Engels (1976) to Gramsci (1971) and Habermas (1989). Moreover, democratizing civil society, as Burawoy (1989) warns us, simply strengthens capitalism.

The Socialists

Elements of the socialists' position are also problematic, in my opinion. All the socialist thinkers reviewed admit to weaknesses in social movements, yet they do not sufficiently compensate for these weaknesses. For example, they all agree that social movements draw participants almost exclusively from the middle classes, and even those who position them within the working class (Navarro, 1988; Philion, 1998; Wilde, 1990) do not articulate how this sector will become revolutionary with all the comforts it has at stake. One of the reasons Marx saw the working class as the privileged agent for socialism was that it had "nothing to lose but its chains." Although elements of the middle class may commit class suicide and join the poor (Freire, 1978), as a whole the class is conservative in terms of economic change. In addition, the NSMs that people speak of (women's, environmental, peace, and identity) are all reformist movements that tend to be temporary and easily co-opted by capitalist democracy. These problems too are not adequately addressed by the socialists. To take just one example from the United States, what could be more temporary than the peace movement? Activists follow the path of U.S. invasions (Vietnam, Grenada, Panama, Iraq, Kosovo) demanding that the United States get out, and when the war ends, so does the movement. Lastly, the dichotomy articulated between Lenin and Gramsci is a false one. A thorough reading of Gramsci shows more convergence with Lenin than divergence from him. It is interesting to see how those who invoke Gramsci's idea of a historical bloc are silent on the political apparatus (the Leninist party) that he saw as the fundamental vehicle possible to achieve this.

I will discuss Gramsci's ideas of the political party, and particularly its role as an agent of radical adult education, in the final chapter. First, however, it is necessary to analyze civil society, a concept I have until now neglected yet that is essential for understanding current radical adult education and left politics.

3

Civil Society within the Marxist Tradition and Beyond

Fundamental to radical pluralism and neo-Marxist socialism is the central role of the theoretical construct of civil society. With antecedents as far back as the Classical Greeks and central to the political philosophies of the Scottish Enlightenment, the concept *civil society* is now the focal point of the theory and practice of a large and growing sector of the left worldwide. In fact, Beckman (1993) says that "the 'liberation of civil society' from the suffocating grip of the state has become the hegemonic ideological project of our time" (p. 20). Beckman, like others (Nzimande & Sikhosana, 1995b; Sachikonye, 1995), cautions that the revival of civil society within the left parallels a similar process among all political sectors and particularly the neoliberal right. There is a convergence of sectors of the right and the left on the need to build or expand civil society, albeit for different goals. To understand how this convergence could happen, it is necessary to examine the current and historical uses of the concept *civil society*. To that end, I will provide a critical review of major theoretical work on the concept. I will begin with a brief analysis of the works of John Locke and Adam Ferguson and then move to the work of Georg Hegel. Because I am particularly interested in the use of the concept of civil society among those of the left today, I will focus on two of the most important figures in the tradition of the left who have written extensively on civil society: Karl Marx and Antonio Gramsci. After examining past conceptualizations of civil society, I will turn to a critical review of the major contemporary theoretical work of the left on civil society. I will argue that contemporary theory can be divided into the radical pluralist (post-Marxist) position—most prominently represented by the influential work of Jean Cohen and Andrew Arato (1992) and the neo-Marxist position of people such as John Keane (1988, 1998). I will conclude with a critique of these contemporary conceptualizations of civil society from what I consider to be a classical Marxist position.

JOHN LOCKE

It is important to understand that John Locke's concept of civil society is tied to his belief in natural law and Christianity. Seligman (1992) says that for Locke, "civil society is . . . the arena where the 'inconveniences' and insufficiencies of the state of nature are rectified through the mutuality of contract and consent. Civil society . . . thus completes the 'perfect freedom' and the 'rights and privileges [enjoyed by men under] the law of nature.' It is but a more perfect form through which the freedom, equality and independence of nature can be realized" (p. 22).

For Locke (1690/1952), the law of Nature "obligates every one, and reason, which is that law, teaches all mankind who will but consult it, that being all equal and independent, no one ought to harm another in his life, health, liberty or possessions; for men being all the workmanship of one omnipotent and infinitely wise Maker, . . . are His property . . . are made to last during His, not one another's, pleasure" (p. 26). From the law of Nature every man has "power not only to reserve his property— that is his life, liberty, and estate . . . but to judge of and punish the breaches of that law by others" (p. 44). A civil society is the state in which men, divinely endowed with inclinations to form societies (p. 42), individually resign their natural power to a higher authority. "Whenever, therefore, any number of men so unite into one society as to quit every one his executive power of the law of Nature, and to resign it to the public, there and there only is a political or civil society" (p. 44). Moreover, the limits of power of a civil society are equivalent to the limits of power of the individual who bequeathed his power to the civil society. "A man . . . cannot subject himself to the arbitrary power of another; and having in the state of Nature no arbitrary power over the life, liberty, or possession of another . . . this is all he doth or can give up to the commonwealth, and by it to the legislative power, so that the legislative can have no more than this" (p. 56).

For Locke, then, civil society is a society that is civil in that it has a political formation in which individuals, who have divinely bestowed characteristics and powers in the state of Nature, mutually decide to relinquish this power to the state for the good of all. It is interesting to see how Locke's position so clearly represents the concrete situation of the nascent English bourgeoisie to which he belonged. He is unable to reject the religious foundations of his thought and base the laws of Nature on pure reason, yet he is clearly articulating the interests of an emerging bourgeois class when he speaks of each individual's right to liberty and property and a state (civil society) that will also guarantee these interests. Of Locke, Engels (Marx & Engels, 1978) said that "both in religion and politics, [he] was the child of the class compromise of 1688" (p. 764). Seen from this perspective, Locke's concept of civil society is fundamentally an effort to provide a philosophical foundation for a form of government that can ensure the "natural" rights of an emerging bourgeois class. It is, then, a revolutionary departure in that it is a direct challenge to the idea that God bestows absolute authority upon a monarchy. For Locke, God bestows authority upon all men, who can freely choose to transfer that authority to a parliament.

The limitations of Locke's thought, resulting from the nature of the society in which he lived, can also be seen in the abstract nature of his ideas. This is most evident in the religious foundation of his thought. Locke speaks of a state of Nature free of coercion in which each individual has equal rights and power, and yet this has nothing to do with the concrete conditions of seventeenth-century England nor to Locke's own employment as the manager of the Earl of Shaftsbury's slave investments (Weatherford, 1988, pp. 31–32). As Seligman (1992) says, "Locke was not positing a historical reality of equality and freedom as the basis of civil society but a theological axiom whose ontological status was not given to empirical evidence or . . . which need not bear any relation to the given historical reality" (p. 24). Born into a society, lacking a systematic and scientific understanding of the natural world and society, Locke could only resort to religion and metaphysics for the foundation of his thought.

ADAM FERGUSON AND THE SCOTTISH ENLIGHTENMENT

As we move to the conceptualization of civil society in the writings of the Scottish Enlightenment, we can, as with Locke, see the reflection of the interests and changing conditions of the bourgeoisie. Like Locke, these writers discuss *civil* society in contrast to *natural* society and therefore do not use civil society to delineate a particular aspect of the social milieu, yet fundamental to civil society is political formation. With the Scottish Enlightenment, however, we see a very interesting departure from Locke in terms of the foundational justification as to why humans form societies. For Locke, God endowed us with a disposition to unite. With the Scottish Enlightenment this becomes mere instinct, and the fundamental reason for humans to form societies is economic exchange. Adam Ferguson (1767/1966) says that "men are united by instinct . . . they act in society from affections of kindness and friendship," and he goes on to say the following:

Mankind . . . [is] devoted to [economic] interest; and this, in all commercial nations, is undoubtedly true; but it does not follow that they are, by their natural dispositions, averse to society and mutual affection: proofs of the contrary remain, even where interest triumphs most. What must we think of the force of that disposition to compassion, to candor, to goodwill, which, notwithstanding the prevailing opinion that the happiness of a man consists in possessing the greatest possible share of riches . . . still keeps the parties who are in competition for those objects on a tolerable footing of amity and leads them to abstain even from their own supposed good, when their seizing it appears in the light of a detriment to others? (p. 35)

For those of the Scottish Enlightenment, civil society is principally the unification of individuals by market exchange. Through this exchange we develop and come to know ourselves as individuals. In civil society "the universal could be found within the particular, the social in the individual, and the public (good) with the private (interest)" (Seligman, 1992, p. 35). If, as we did with Locke, we view philosophy as dialectically related to the concrete conditions of material life, we see, in a society developing a scientific understanding of the world, religious explanations becoming less prominent in the more advanced philosophy of the time. Moreover, there is an effort to empirically justify claims, as we see with the writing of Ferguson. Yet, the analysis is one-sided. Ferguson (1767/1966), for example, says that "happiness of individuals is the great end of civil society" (p. 58). In the realm of exchange, which is central to Ferguson's civil society, who achieves happiness? Obviously, exchange is rarely a win-win situation. For an up-and-coming class, wholly self-conscious of its progressive role in the defeat of feudalism and its growing political and economic power, happiness can be the goal of exchange. What is lacking here, however, is an analysis of the nature of the relations among real individuals in the arena of exchange. As Marx (1959) says of the political economy of the Scottish Enlightenment, "political economy proceeds from the fact of private property, but it does not explain it to us" (p. 64). Specifically, beyond the "happiness" of the capitalist in the process of exchange is the entire process of alienation directly experienced by the laborer. This fact, and its origins, is absent in the conceptualization of civil society in the Scottish Enlightenment but not in the work of Hegel, who would be the next major philosopher to deal extensively with the concept of civil society.

GEORG HEGEL

With Georg Hegel, the concept of civil society takes on a very different meaning, compared to the concept with Locke and the Scottish Enlightenment. This is due, in large part, to Hegel's dialectical and historical method, albeit wholly idealist. Hegel analyzes civil society historically as developing out of the family. Furthermore, civil society is not, as with the Scottish Enlightenment, the realization of the unity of the particular with the universal, but constitutes this unity in alienated form.

In the *Philosophy of Right*, Hegel (1821/1967) posits two principles of civil society. First, "the concrete person, who is himself the object of his particular aims, is . . . a totality of wants and a mixture of a caprice and physical necessity" (p. 122). Second, "the particular person is essentially so related to other particular persons that each establishes himself and finds satisfaction by means of the others, and at the same time purely and simply by means of the form of universality" (pp. 122–123). Marx (1959) was very aware of how much he drew from Hegel and commented that the importance of Hegel lay in the fact that he "grasps the essence of *labor* and comprehends objective man . . . as the outcome of man's *own labor*" (p. 140). We see this very clearly when Hegel (1821/1967) says that "the division of labor . . . , this abstraction of one man's skill and means of production from another's, completes and makes necessary everywhere the dependence of men on one another and their reciprocal relation in the satisfaction of their other needs" (p. 129).

At this point we see similarities between Hegel and the Scottish Enlightenment in that the universal interest of all is tied to the particular interest of each individual operating in civil society. For Hegel, however, the process of the realization of the universal Idea is not ultimately in civil society but in the state.

In these circumstances [relation of the particular and universal in civil society], the interest of the Idea—an interest of which these members of civil society are as such unconscious—lies in the process whereby their singularity and their natural condition are raised, as a result of the necessities imposed by nature as well as of arbitrary needs, to formal freedom and formal universality of knowing and willing—the process whereby their particularity is educated up to subjectivity (pp. 124–125)

For Hegel, education plays a fundamental role in the actualization of the Idea in the state. Through education the mind is trained to see that the immediate and particular can be realized only in relation to the universal actualized in the state. "The final purpose of education, therefore, is liberation and the struggle for a higher liberation still; education is the absolute transition from an ethical substantiality which is immediate and natural to the one which is intellectual and so both infinitely subjective and lofty enough to have attained universality of form" (p. 125).

Civil society is the realm of the particular in which only through the aggregate of individuals is the realization of the interests of each individual achieved. The realization or actualization of this universal Idea, alienated in civil society, culminates in the state. "Hence, the sphere of civil society passes over into the state. . . . The state is the actuality of the ethical Idea" (pp. 154–155). The idealism of Hegel prevents him from positing true liberation from the alienation in civil society. For Hegel, "the whole *history of the alienation-process* and the whole *process of the retraction* of the alienation is therefore nothing but the *history of the production* of abstract (i.e., absolute) thought—of logical, speculative thought" (Marx, 1959, p. 138). We can attribute Hegel's emphasis on education as the tool of liberation to his idealism, as well. That we can change the world by changing our perceptions of it is idealist. Lacking is the unity of education, ideology, and theory with practical struggle— praxis. That the state is the overcoming of the alienation of civil society was wholly and rightfully critiqued by Marx. For the philosophical and young Marx, the state is simply one more form of alienation of our own capacities to supervise and direct our own affairs; and for Marx, the political economist, the state is an instrument of domination created by the ruling class to achieve its goals.

Hegel does, however, posit civil society historically. This was an advance for social theory. No longer was civil society viewed as natural or static. Moreover, Hegel provided a method of inquiry that, when stripped of its idealist shell, provides a powerful tool for Marx to develop a robust and unsurpassed understanding of *bürgerliche gesellschaft*— "bourgeois," or civil, society.

KARL MARX

Karl Marx's use of the term *civil society* appears early in his writing, when he is still formulating his materialist positions in contrast to the idealism of Hegel and the Young Hegelians. In fact, Marx's famous inversion of Hegel can be seen in how he conceptualizes the nature of civil society in opposition to Hegel. "The idea [with Hegel] is made the subject and the *actual* relation of family and civil society to the state is conceived as its *internal imaginary* activity. Family and civil society are the premises of the state; they are genuinely active elements, but in speculative philosophy [Hegel] things are inverted. . . . They are the driving force. According to Hegel, they are, on the contrary, *produced* by the actual idea" (Marx, in Marx & Engels, 1978, p. 16).

Jarvis (1993) argues that "it is impossible to separate civil society from the state" (p. 6). This is clearly the case for Marx in *On the Jewish Question* and in his later writings as well. In *On the Jewish Question*, Marx (1844/ 1975) is grappling with several issues relating to the state and civil society that we have already seen in Locke, the Scottish Enlightenment, and Hegel: the relationship between the state and civil society, the idea of the state of nature, and the nature of political rights. Unlike all the previous theorists, however, Marx deals with the concrete—humans as they actually live their lives and not in the ideal or abstract.

Marx, like Hegel, views civil society historically—again, not in the abstract, but as it actually emerges from the real activity of individuals. Marx argues that in feudalism, society was directly political. "The elements of civil life, . . . property, or the family, or the mode of labor, were raised to the level of elements of political life in the form of seigniory, estates, and corporations" (p. 165). The bourgeois revolutions of the eighteenth century *"abolish* the *political character of civil society"* (p. 166). The bourgeois state embodies "political man." This state, argues Marx in direct opposition to Hegel, is not the concrete realization of human liberation. "By freeing himself *politically,* man frees himself in a *roundabout way,* through an intermediary. . . . The state is the intermediary between man and man's freedom" (p. 152). Moreover, "in the state . . . man is . . . the imaginary member of an illusory sovereignty, is deprived of his real individual life and endowed with an unreal universality" (p. 154).

If the bourgeois revolutions abolish the political character of civil society, how, then, do humans appear in civil society? Marx answers this question and implicitly shows the error of Locke and the Scottish Enlightenment's views of civil society. "Man as a member of civil society, *unpolitical* man, inevitably appears . . . as the *natural* man. The *droits de l'homme* appears as *droits naturels,* because *conscious activity* is concentrated on the *political act. Egoistic* man is the *passive* result of the dissolved society, a result that is simply *found* in *existence,* an object of *immediate certainty,* therefore a *natural* object" (p. 167). Marx, unlike those who came before him, is not fooled by these appearances. There is nothing "natural" or spontaneous about the emergence of the bourgeois state out of the real activity of individuals in civil society. "Political life [the bourgeois state] declares itself to be a mere *means,* whose purpose is the life of civil society" (p. 164). Marx more concretely identifies how the state becomes a means for civil society when he analyzes the essence of the rights granted by the constitutions of the bourgeois state.

The right of man to liberty is based not on the association of man with man, but on the separation of man from man. . . . The practical application of man's right to liberty is man's right to *private property.* . . . The right of man to private property is, therefore, the right to enjoy one's property and to dispose of it at one's discretion . . . , without regard to other men, independently of society, the right of self interest. This individual liberty and its application form the basis of civil society. It makes every man see in other men not the *realization* of his own freedom, but the *barrier* to it. . . . *Security* is the highest social concept of civil society. (pp. 162–163)

We see in *On the Jewish Question* all the fundamental components of Marx's analysis of civil society and its relation to the state that pervade his subsequent writing. There is, however, a certain abstractness in Marx's analysis in *On the Jewish Question* due to the philosophical nature of his analysis at this point in his development. The specific class character of the state and civil society is not fully developed in *On the Jewish Question*. This is understandable considering the fact that he only begins, along with Engels, to develop in earnest his materialist conception of history three years later in *The German Ideology* (Marx & Engels, 1976).

Civil society embraces the whole material intercourse of individuals within a definite stage of the development of productive forces. It embraces the whole commercial and industrial life of a given stage and, insofar, transcends the state and the nation, though, on the other hand again, it must assert itself in its external relations as nationality and internally must organize itself as state. The term "civil society" [*bürgerliche gesellschaft*] emerged in the eighteenth century, when property relations had already extricated themselves from the ancient and medieval community. Civil society as such develops with the bourgeoisie; the social organization evolving directly out of production and intercourse, which in all ages forms the basis of the state and of the rest of the idealistic superstructure, has, however, always been designated by the same name. (p. 98)

We see in *The German Ideology* the impact of the historical and political economic studies that Marx, at that point, was still just beginning. Marx and Engels clarify civil society as a sociological construct ("the whole material intercourse of individuals within a definite stage of the development of productive forces") and as an ideologically charged political term with a specific historical origin (" 'civil society' emerged in the eighteenth century, when property relations had already extricated themselves from the ... medieval community"). It is interesting to note how the former usage of the term (as sociological construct), which is central to Marx's methodology of historical materialism, belies the latter charges of economic determinism in Marx. Marx views (civil) society as a dialectical *totality* of base and superstructure.

For Marx, capitalism, in which we can first begin to speak of a civil society, emerges in the sixteenth century and blossoms in the eighteenth. Philosophers at that time (Locke and the Scottish Enlightenment) were confronted with a world in which for the first time one can see individuals (particularly the bourgeoisie) seemingly free of the feudal and ancient bonds that tied them to the land and the lord in a limited existence. These philosophers saw this phenomenon not as a product of a historical development but as an ideal, natural condition. This, they believed, was the way that humans really were, in essence. What they failed to realize (unlike Marx) is that this appearance of individuality is the result of a social process of production. We stand as seemingly independent individuals because at our disposal (to various degrees) are all the fruits (past and present) of a vast and ever developing "network" of millions actively engaged and related to one another in production. To understand this network, this mode of production, was the key to an understanding of civil society, and that was precisely what Marx set out to do in his political economic studies that produced *Capital* in 1867. This was not, however, merely an academic exercise for Marx. For "only when man has recognized and organized his *'forces propres'* as *social* forces, and consequently no longer separates social power from himself in the shape of *political* power, only then will human emancipation have been accomplished" (Marx, 1844/1975, p. 168). More concretely stated, human emancipation is the overcoming of the alienation represented in the separation of political power (the state) and the social relations of production. A state is only necessary in a social formation based on exploitation. "The state arose from the need to keep class antagonisms in check, [and] it is normally the state of the . . . economically dominant class" (Engels, 1891/1978, p. 208). Therefore, the proletariat, "a class in civil society, that is not of civil society . . . a social group that is the dissolution of all social groups, of a sphere that has a universal character because of its universal sufferings" (Marx, 1977b, p. 72), is a truly revolutionary class. No reforms eliminate the exploitation of the proletariat. When those who produce take control of all the means of production and in the process eliminate the separation of state and civil society, and thereby the state itself, only then can we speak of human emancipation.

Marx realized that the process of revolution occurred when the social relations of production became fetters on the developing forces of production because of his analysis of the transformation from feudalism to capitalism. His studies of capitalism and concrete social change (the Paris Commune) propelled him to anticipate the nature of the transition from capitalism to socialism as necessitating a violent seizure of the means of production and the bourgeois state by an organized working class who would then have to dismantle this state and create a transitionary "workers' state," or dictatorship of the proletariat. Marx, from his historical position, could not envision the full potential of the bourgeoisie to maintain hegemony over the working class. The study of the resilience of capitalist hegemony would be left to future Marxists such as Antonio Gramsci.

ANTONIO GRAMSCI

Antonio Gramsci made this hegemony the centerpiece of his use of the concept of civil society, the study of which he dedicated himself to after his imprisonment. Elements of his analysis of hegemony can be found in his pre-prison writings such as "The Southern Question" (see Buci-Glucksmann, 1980), but it is in the *Prison Notebooks* that Gramsci profoundly studies the question of hegemony. Two points should be made about Gramsci's study of hegemony. First, the concept of hegemony within Marxism was not original to Gramsci. Gramsci (1971) himself recognized that "the greatest modern theoretician of the philosophy of praxis [Lenin], on the terrain of political struggle and organization and with a political terminology, gave new weight—in opposition to the various 'economist' tendencies—to the front of cultural struggle, and constructed the doctrine of hegemony as a complement to the theory of the state-as-force" (p. 56). Secondly, Gramsci's (1994a) study of hegemony was part of his larger study of the role of intellectuals who operated in what he called civil society, or the area of the state associated with consent, as opposed to political society, or "state-as-force."

The research I have done on the intellectuals is very broad. . . . My study also leads to certain definitions of the concept of the State, that is usually understood as political Society (or dictatorship, or coercive apparatus meant to mold the popular mass in accordance with the type of production and economy at a given moment) and not as a balance between the political Society and civil Society (or the hegemony of a social group over the entire national society, exercised through the so-called private organizations, such as the Church, the unions, the schools, etc.), and it is within the civil society that intellectuals operate. (pp. 66–67)

In the above quote, we have a concise outline of Gramsci's concept of civil society that differs from the way Marx uses the concept. For Gramsci, civil society is superstructural; he uses it to describe a particular aspect of state power—hegemony. It must be emphasized, in anticipation of subsequent theorists of civil society, that Gramsci does not posit civil society as a social realm autonomous from the state, nor from the social relations of production. This point is of extreme importance because of its relevance to political practice. Gramsci (1971) says, "the 'spontaneous' consent given by the great masses of the population to the general direction imposed on social life by the dominant fundamental group; this consent *is 'historically' caused by the prestige (and consequent confidence) which the dominant group enjoys because of its position and function in the world of production* [italics added]" (p. 12). Moreover, he says that "for though hegemony is ethical-political, it must also be economic, must necessarily be based on the decisive function exercised by the leading group in the decisive nucleus of economic activity" (p. 161). We must never forget that Gramsci was a Marxist, and therefore he understood that "the class which is the ruling material force of society is at the same time its ruling intellectual force." In addition, it is important to realize that, for

Gramsci, civil society (superstructural) was not the exclusive domain for the creation of hegemony. The ruling class can also exert hegemony at the point of production. In discussing Fordism, Gramsci says, "Hegemony here is born in the factory and requires for its exercise only a minute quantity of professional political and ideological intermediaries. The phenomenon ... is nothing but the form taken by this 'rationalized' society in which the 'structure' dominates the superstructures more immediately and in which the latter are also 'rationalized' " (pp. 285–286).

If the ruling class exerts hegemony in civil society or at the point of production, how does Gramsci envision the movement of the working class? Interpretations of this question have led to so much distortion that it is difficult to see the actual ideas of Gramsci in the secondary literature. On this point, Phelps (1995) says, "Gramsci has become safe, tame, denatured, a wisp of his revolutionary self. Academics seeking to justify their retreat into highly abstruse theories have created fanciful illusions about their 'counterhegemonic' activity. They have created a mythical Gramsci who holds views he never did, including an opposition to revolutionary socialist organizations of the sort that he, following upon Lenin, held indispensable" (p. 54). Essentially, the distortions of Gramsci come largely from radical pluralists who hold positions in institutions of civil society—such as schools, universities, community-based organizations—who want to believe that their educational work creates organic intellectuals and that reform-oriented organizing within social movements is counter-hegemonic political work, faithful to Gramsci. The fundamental problems with this are twofold. First, Gramsci was not a radical pluralist. He was a communist who believed in the absolute necessity of a revolutionary vanguard party of the working class. "The Communist Party is the instrument and the historical form of the process of inner liberation through which the worker is transformed from *executor* to *initiator*, from mass to *leader* and *guide*, from pure brawn to a brain and a will" (Gramsci, 1994b, p. 191). Second, the problem with attributing the concept of counter-hegemony to Gramsci is that he never used the term. Again, this is an invention and a distortion on the part of radical pluralists who use Gramsci to justify radical pluralist politics. An excellent example of this, as we have seen in the last chapter, is Carl Boggs's *The Two Revolutions*. In the preface, Boggs (1984) says that because Gramsci had to write under censorship and use many euphemisms, "many of the concepts, terms, and premises he employed were exceedingly vague or lacking in clear definition or application" (p. xi).

It is wishful thinking to say that Gramsci's ideas were vague. They are vague only for a radical pluralist reading of them. Why use "counterhegemony?" It speaks to a defensive, reformist politics within a sociological paradigm that sees civil society as a sphere largely independent of the state and the economy. Boggs and the rest of the radical pluralists do not need to put words in Gramsci's mouth; they can use Gramsci's own terms: *hegemony of the proletariat* or *proletarian hegemony.* "The Turin communists had raised in concrete terms the question of the 'hegemony of the proletariat'; in other words, the question of the social basis of the proletarian dictatorship and the workers' State. For the proletariat to become the ruling, the dominant, class, it must succeed in creating a system of class alliances which allow it to mobilize the majority of the working population against capitalism and the bourgeois state" (Gramsci, 1994b, p. 316). Is this "vague" or "lacking in clear . . . application"? I do not think so. For Gramsci, the vanguard party—a party made up largely of working-class people and some middle-class intellectuals who have committed class suicide—must lead and direct the spontaneous actions of a broad spectrum of people from the oppressed classes toward an assault on the bourgeois state. We see from Gramsci's own practice that the fundamental place for this type of activity was, for him, at the point of production—the factory councils, not in civil society. Gramsci saw the factory councils as the Italian version of Soviets—organs of people's power that would become the workers' state.

Having reviewed the positions of Marx and Gramsci, the two most important thinkers on civil society in the tradition of the left, I will now turn to an analysis of contemporary work on civil society, which I see as divided into two broad positions: a post-Marxist, radical pluralist position (exemplified by Cohen and Arato) and a neo-Marxist socialist position (exemplified by Keane).

JEAN COHEN AND ANDREW ARATO

The work of Jean Cohen and Andrew Arato on civil society, culminating in their lengthy book *Civil Society and Political Theory*, is arguably the most influential book on this subject today among radical pluralists. Cohen and Arato (1992) define civil society in the following way:

We understand "civil society" as a sphere of social interaction between economy and state, composed above all of the intimate sphere (especially the family), the sphere of associations . . . , social movements, and forms of public communication. Modern civil society is created through forms of self-constitution and self-mobilization. It is institutionalized and generalized through laws, and especially subjective rights, that stabilize social differentiation. While the self-creative and institutionalized dimensions can exist separately, in the long term both independent action and institutionalization are necessary for the reproduction of civil society. (p. ix)

I find the perspective of Cohen and Arato to be inadequate and counterproductive as a theory that can guide political practice aimed at human emancipation for three main reasons. First, they write from what is ultimately an idealist perspective. Because they do not come from a historical materialist perspective, they can ignore social reality for the construction of models and ideal types as guides for understanding and changing reality. We see their idealism in various instances. In the preface, they argue that "only a reconstruction involving a three-part model distinguishing civil society from both state and economy has a chance ... to renew its critical potential under liberal democracies" (p. ix). Theorizing about social change is not about pulling possible models out of thin air, but analyzing the real conditions that have historically developed. If Cohen and Arato had done this, they would know that it flies in the face of historical reality to talk about a social realm separated from the state and the economy. This is simply idealist wishful thinking. We see this again when they discuss the relationship between property and rights in civil society, which Marx so clearly analyzed in *On the Jewish Question* and in *The German Ideology*.

Only if one construes property to be not simply a key right but the core of the conception of rights—only, that is, if one places the philosophy of possessive individualism at the heart of one's conception of civil society and then reduces civil to bourgeois society—does the rights thesis come to be defined in this way. If, however, one develops a more complex model of civil society ... rights do not only secure negative liberty, the autonomy of private, disconnected individuals. They also secure the autonomous (freed from state control) *communicative interaction* of individuals with one another in the public and private spheres of civil society. (Cohen & Arato, 1992, p. 22)

Calling a theory "more complex" does not make it fit a historical reality that refutes it. Their "model" of a civil society is simply not the civil society in which they or we live. The bourgeoisie that created it had "the philosophy of possessive individualism" at the heart of its practice. To say it could or might be otherwise does not change the historical development of reality. Even Habermas (1989), from which Cohen and Arato took the idea of "communicative interaction," recognized the fact that the civil society of the bourgeois public sphere was a conscious creation of the bourgeoisie during its political ascendancy.

Second, it is interesting to see how the radical pluralists attempt to get around Marx's analysis of civil society that wholly refutes the idea that there can be a civil society autonomous from the state and economy. In the case of Cohen and Arato, their strategy is to simply ignore the specifics of Marx's analysis of civil society. In a book of nearly 800 pages that contains a review of major theories of civil society that covers 262 pages, Cohen and Arato dedicate *one sentence* to directly addressing Marx's concept of civil society in their review of Hegel: "There is no need to repeat Marx's brilliant 1843 critique of the pretensions of Hegel's view of the universal estate, which pinpointed its particular interests and status consciousness" (p. 103). Of course they do not outline Marx's "brilliant" critique, because it is utterly devastating to Hegel's and their own idealist and ultimately conservative concept of civil society. They cannot include Marx in a discussion because, as they admit, "Marx stressed the negative aspects of civil society, its atomistic and dehumanizing features; but in so doing, he managed to deepen the analysis of the economic dimensions of the *systems of needs* and went far beyond Hegel in analyzing the social consequences of capitalist development" (p. 17). Given this admission, they refuse to deal with Marx because few if any of their beloved social movements fundamentally challenge the root of the "social consequences of capitalist development," and Cohen and Arato, quite frankly, are not much concerned with the root cause of these consequences, for theirs is a capitalist, bourgeois, democratic project.

Third, as just stated, Cohen and Arato's political strategy is wholly reformist. It is in no way whatsoever a challenge to capitalism, and, in fact, it advocates the unfettering of its supposed economic efficiency. Therefore, it cannot be an emancipatory project. The most obvious example of their reformist nature comes in a footnote to Chapter 11 in a discussion of civil disobedience and the economy as outlined by Michael Walzer.

Corporate power is exercised over employee-subjects in ways not dissimilar from those of authoritarian states. . . . The strike . . . was for a long time the most common form of working-class civil disobedience. Walzer argues that such actions, even if they appear as revolutionary in that they aim at altering the distribution of power within the corporation, fall within the limits of civility so long as the revolution is not aimed at the state itself. . . . We agree with this argument with one proviso: *economic efficiency should not be sacrificed in toto to democratic pressure* [italics added]. (Cohen & Arato, 1992, p. 741)

Clearly, then, Cohen and Arato attempt to infuse idealist, reform-oriented theory into the current debate over which way the left should proceed. In the end, their theory is useless for anyone interested in emancipatory struggles. The state and the economy must be the main targets of a left serious about social change, and not ignored, as Cohen and Arato ultimately argue. That is why the left must include, but go beyond, the narrowness of the NSMs that Cohen and Arato advocate, precisely because they do not directly challenge the state or economy.

JOHN KEANE

Whereas Cohen and Arato represent a post-Marxist, radical pluralist perspective on civil society, John Keane (1988) is representative of a neo-

Marxist socialist perspective that is critical of the destructiveness of capitalist production but is wary of the dismantling of the bourgeois state. Furthermore, he argues that the left must reassess the utility of classical Marxism's analysis of the state and civil society. "The meaning of socialism can and must be altered radically—into a synonym for the democratization of civil society and the state" (p. xiii). I will begin my discussion of Keane by outlining his conceptualization of civil society and the way in which he envisions social change. As a way of concluding this section and this chapter, I will engage in an analysis and critique of what Keane sees as serious limitations in Marx's analysis of the state and civil society. I will discuss this at length, not in an effort to preserve Marx as sacred dogma but to show that neither the radical pluralists nor the neo-Marxists, as represented in what I believe are the respective positions' most sophisticated presentations in Cohen and Arato and Keane, have provided a convincing argument for abandoning the basic tenets of classical Marxism in terms of the state and civil society.

Keane (1988) defines civil society as "an aggregate of institutions whose members are engaged primarily in a complex of non-state activities—economic and cultural production, household life and voluntary associations—and who in this way preserve and transform their identity by exercising all sorts of pressures or controls upon state institutions" (p. 14). From this definition Keane outlines the following "socialist" strategy that, simply put, entails an organized civil society that keeps the state "civil" and a sympathetic state that keeps civil society "civil" in a perpetual "tug-of-war" between the state and civil society. Let's let Keane explain himself.

Democratization—the "road to socialism"—would mean attempting to redefine the boundaries between civil society and the state through two interdependent and simultaneous processes: the expansion of social equality and liberty, and the restructuring and democratizing of state institutions. Two conditions would be necessary for the successful enactment of these processes. First, the power not only of private capital and the state, but also of white, heterosexual, male citizens over (what remains of) civil society would need to be curtailed through social struggles and public policy initiatives that enabled citizens, acting together in "socialable" public sphere, to strive to equal power, and to maximize their capacity to play an active part in civil society.

Secondly, state institutions would have to become more accountable to civil society by having their functions ... recast. ... State institutions must be understood as devices for enacting legislation, promulgating new policies, containing inevitable conflicts between particular interests within well-defined legal limits, and for preventing civil society from falling victim to new forms of inequality and tyranny. (pp. 14–15)

Keane sees an alliance between renewed political parties operating in the state and NSMs operating in civil society as the agent of this strategy.

He believes that this strategy would overcome the problems of anarcho-syndicalism, which leaves civil society to fend for itself, and state socialism, which dominates civil society. "It rejects the assumption that the state could ever legitimately replace civil society or vice versa" (p. 14).

In his more recent work, *Civil Society: Old Images, New Visions* (1998), Keane holds fast to the state–civil society tug-of-war strategy. The major difference, however, paralleling the "retreat from class" that we saw with Carl Boggs in Chapter 2, is that building civil society is now merely a "road to democracy" and not the "road to socialism," as in 1988. "The purpose of democratization [no longer a road to socialism] cannot be synonymous with the extension of total state power into the non-state sphere of civil society. Conversely, . . . democratization cannot be defined as the abolition of the state and the building of spontaneous agreement among citizens living within civil society" (p. 9). In addition, the tug-of-war strategy now includes the market. "Where there are no markets, civil societies find it impossible to survive. But the converse rule also applies: where there is no civil society, there can be no markets" (p. 19).

It is curious how the left looks at history and seems to want to punish itself for "trying to go too far" when we have rarely ever gone far enough. The problem with Keane's strategy is that in an effort to be more "realistic" by trying to be less ambitious, it becomes less realistic and more utopian. The problem, for example, during the Allende years in Chile was not that the left was too revolutionary—and therefore brought on the full force of reaction, as many civil society advocates claim—but that it was not revolutionary enough, in the sense that it did not do away with the right's hold on the military. This is also the problem with Keane; the right would never permit this idea of constant state–civil society stalemate that he thinks will prevent anarchistic or statist excesses. In essence, my argument, paralleling that of Ehrenberg (1992), is that socialists of late have not suffered from an excess of "orthodoxy" but from "insufficient fidelity to its roots" (p. 2). The theoretical work of Marx and Engels and Lenin is of a democracy far more egalitarian than the narrow bourgeois democracy advocated by neo-Marxists and radical pluralists. Keane, however, disagrees and outlines three areas in which he believes that Marx's analysis of the state and civil society are inadequate.

First, Keane (1988) says that Marx's analysis of civil society is one-dimensional because, though emphasizing the historic specificity of civil society and the importance of production, it "is blind to the ways in which the emergence of the modern bourgeois mode of production was facilitated by the *prior* development of social organs . . . of the decaying feudal order" (p. 58). Marx—not to mention numerous latter Marxist historians—in Part 8 of *Capital, Vol. I* and also in *The German Ideology* specifically addresses the emergence of capitalist civil society from the feudal order. Keane further argues that "the Marxian interpretation fails to see that bourgeois civil societies, past or present, cannot be understood purely and simply as spheres of egoism, private property and class conflict" (p. 58). To argue that capitalism is something other than a system based on private property, egoism, and class conflict is wishful thinking. That there are certain "rights" and democratic guarantees is wholly the result of fierce class struggles (see Aptheker, 1967, for this perspective applied to the history of the United States).

Second, Keane (1988) says that "the Marxian theory generally defends a conception of the state as little more than an arena within which societal conflicts are fought out, interests mediated, and the ensuring results authoritatively confirmed" (p. 59). Keane provides no evidence to show that this theory of the state is incorrect. He merely argues that "a contemporary democratic theory of civil society and the state . . . must reject this society-centered approach and its one-sided assumption that 'political conditions are only the official expression of civil society' " (p. 59). Of course he must reject Marx's analysis of the state, for if that analysis, based on a careful historical study of how it actually came to be, is essentially accurate, then Keane's "friendly state that oversees civil society" strategy falls to pieces. To argue that "state policies often successfully pursue courses of action at variance with dominant social classes" (p. 61) is proof of Marx's error ignores Marx's own analysis of temporary contradictions with the state and the bourgeoisie (as in Marx's *The Eighteenth Brumaire* [1852/1974]), and the fact that these anomalies are always the result of compromise forced upon the ruling class by class struggle.

Third, Keane argues that Marx's analysis of the abolition of the state by the working class "failed to recognize that the democratic potential of workers within any particular country depends upon such factors as historical traditions, the structure of industrial relations, state strategies, and their ability to form bounds of solidarity with other groups within civil society" (p. 62). This claim ignores Marx's political writings on Ireland, the Paris Commune, Bonapartism, and so forth, in which he dealt concretely with all these factors, including alliances. Furthermore, Lenin (1902/1970) too dealt both theoretically and politically with the importance of alliances. In fact, alliances were an essential prerequisite for a vanguard party. Keane also says that "Marx . . . failed to consider whether social victories of the proletariat might have led along the lines of a more radicalized, more property-sensitive version of Tocqueville's model of a democratic state" (p. 60). Quite to the contrary, Marx not only did not fail to consider this, he also did not fail to witness this in the Paris Commune. A relevant important conclusion that he drew from this he placed in a preface to *The Communist Manifesto*. "One thing especially was proved by the Commune, viz., that 'the working class cannot simply lay hold of the ready-made State machinery, and wield it for its own purposes'" (Marx & Engels, 1848/1948, p. 7). Finally, Keane says that "Marx's vision of a conflict- and power-free communist society failed to acknowledge that state institutions would always be required to some degree in complex, post-capitalist systems" (p. 60). Again Keane is mistaken. Marx's idea of the dictatorship of the proletariat is precisely a postcapitalist state. Moreover, Marx, unlike Keane, was very specific about the class nature of this state. In regard to the phase of communism beyond the dictatorship of the proletariat, Marx was less exact because he dealt not in utopian speculation but in an analysis of the concrete. To predict the specific structures of society beyond the phase of the dictatorship of the proletariat was, for Marx, speculation. Marx did discuss the transitional phase between capitalism and socialism because one could concretely see the emergence of socialism in "the womb of capitalism."

CONCLUSION

In the sections covering contemporary conceptualizations of civil society, I have tried to show how neither the radical pluralist nor the neo-Marxist position posits a theory and practice of civil society that goes beyond classical Marxism in understanding the historical development of civil society or the paths toward its negation. I am not alone in this position. Sachikonye (1995) argues that much of current civil society theory is based on a "minimalist" definition of democracy in the tradition of Western liberalism. Western liberal democracy posits a separation of the state, society, and the economy and guarantees only civil rights. This liberal notion of democracy, with its emphasis on the separation of state and civil society, is the ideological foundation of neoliberal structural adjustment programs. Civil society theory, then, plays into the hand of structural adjustment schemes when it too champions the irrelevance of the state and the importance of civil society. "In an effort to delegitimize the principal ideological rival—economic nationalism—neo-liberals seek to delegitimize the state, the main locus of nationalist aspirations and resistance to the neo-liberal project. In order to undercut the claims by the state to represent the nation, its alien nature is emphasized; its retrogressiveness is explained in terms of separation from civil society" (p. 9). It must be noted that the left also falls for this trap in the North. Civil society advocates in the corporate community-based organization sector have championed privatization (structural adjustment) schemes in the United States as well. From self-management of public housing and public schools to the privatization of welfare and adult education, sectors of the left, raising slogans of community control and empowerment, have played an integral role in furthering the state's abandonment of guaranteeing basic social services under the guise of promoting personal and community responsibility.

Nzimande and Sikhosana (1995b) agree that civil society theory has uncritically abandoned the Marxist analysis of civil society.

Arguments for an autonomous "civil society" are the greatest disservice to Marxism itself. With a stroke of the pen, they wipe out the entire Marxist critique of liberal and bourgeois democracy. It is as if Marxist theory had not undertaken more than a century of critique of capitalism and its political institutions. All of a sudden, without much references to these debates we are told that the Marxist mistake was to throw away the baby with the bathwater (i.e., throwing away capitalism with its liberal freedoms), *as if socialism is simply an incremental building upon liberal bourgeois freedoms!* [italics added] (p. 37)

Nzimande and Sikhosana are right to point out that socialism is not an expansion of bourgeois democracy. The expansion of bourgeois democracy is exactly the problem with the concept of "counter-hegemony"—a definitive bourgeois political practice. When Gramsci spoke of proletarian hegemony, he meant the building of anticapitalist, proletarian organizations. Nzimande and Sikhosana (1995a) clarify this distinction when they discuss the difference between "mass organizations"—issue-oriented and often temporary social movements—and "organs of people's power," which are about "the fundamental and revolutionary transformation of society, . . . the transfer of power to the people and . . . the wielding of state power" (p. 59).

The most common critique against classical Marxism today is that it does not account for the most visible form of struggle—social movements. As we saw in the previous chapter, it is argued that social movements, seen as operating in "civil society," have replaced the working class as the historic agents of social change. What this position fails to realize is that "much of the devaluation of class and the de-radicalization of class in academic debates is the outcome of current capitalist practices. What has been seen is the reduction of the organized industrial proletariat. . . . The working class has not vanished, it has been reconstituted in larger numbers" (Chandhoke, 1990, p. 1725). Indeed, the reduction of working-class militancy and organization is the result of mistakes made by working-class leadership and the brutal class struggle waged on the part of capital. Capital has used every weapon at its disposal to fragment and weaken the working class. That NSMs have emerged among largely petit-bourgeois elements is merely a reflection of the fact that this stratum, too, is feeling the effects of class warfare that destroys our communities, environment, and security. Classical Marxism never denied the fact that the petite bourgeoisie would struggle for its own interests. Quite the contrary; this class is pivotal. It is precisely with this class, along with the peasantry (where appropriate), that alliances must be formed in order that a working-class party can be a vanguard (Lenin) and lead (Gramsci) the fight against capitalism. Classical Marxism does maintain, however, that the working class must be at the forefront because only the working class is a universal class or a class whose emancipation requires a fundamentally new society; without working-class leadership we are condemned to petit-bourgeois, reform-oriented social movements and limiting civil society theory.

My focus in the last two chapters has been on the politics of social movements and the development and use of the concept of civil society among certain sectors of the left. In the next chapter I will turn to an analysis of these issues specifically within the left in adult education. It has been necessary to cover this terrain outside the field of adult education because, as we shall see, it is precisely these debates that shape the discussion of social movements and civil society within adult education. This is not to say, however, that adult education has nothing original to contribute to the discussion.

4

Adult Education, Social Movements, and Civil Society

"This is a great discovery, education is politics." With this statement, Paulo Freire (Shor & Freire, 1987, p. 46) unmasks one of the fundamental aspects of adult education and of education in general. From this analysis, the question of the relationship between adult education and the transformation of society becomes critical. We witness this fact in the growing importance given to the relationship among adult education, social movements, and civil society in the literature since the wide dissemination of Freire's ideas beginning in the mid-1970s. Ironically, it is interesting to see how what was once implicit and taken for granted is now the focus of much debate within the field. Specifically, if we take a long and broad view of adult education, beyond the standard histories (Knowles, 1977; Stubblefield, 1988), we realize that those involved in various social movements have assumed that education was an essential part of social change, without the intervention of professional adult educators. To take one specific example, Foner (1947) discusses how in the 1860s, Uriah S. Stephens, one of the founders of the Knights of Labor, believed that "education ... would play a large part in achieving the immediate and ultimate objects of the Knights of Labor by breaking down prejudice ... which still divided the working class" (p. 436). Clearly, as Hall (1978), among others (Faris, 1986; Heaney, 1993; Lovett, 1988b; Lovett, Clarke, & Kilmurray, 1983; Rubenson, 1989; Schied, 1993; Selman, 1990), believes, "involvement, participation, political action is not new to adult education; it has been a fundamental principle for centuries" (p. 8).

The relationship to social movements is fundamental to how people view the current status of the field of education and its revitalization. Kastner (1990) says that working in social movements can help adult education to meet its goals of enhancing lifelong education if we see these movements as essential to good citizenship. Those who are concerned with issues of social justice, for example, see the current interest in social movements and civil society as a revitalization of our roots. As Collins (1991) argues, "in making vocation a paramount concern, we are not introducing a radically new orientation to the field of adult education but, rather, one that has been pushed to the margins by obsession with pedagogical technique and management by objectives" (p. 41).

The debates over social movements and civil society within the field, then, are vital to the theory and practice of contemporary adult education. These internal debates, however, do not take place in isolation from the wider debates over social movements and civil society and the nature of the political left. In fact, the wider debates, with the dichotomy between radical pluralists and socialists that we saw in Chapters 2 and 3, in sociology, political science, and alternative politics largely shape the debates within adult education.

The dichotomy between radical pluralists and socialists permeates the literature on social movements and civil society in adult education, which addresses four issues of specific concern to adult education. First, some have addressed the question of whether education itself can change society. Second, many have tried to address the question of the nature of the education that takes place in social movements. Third, the issue of the potential of NSMs to change society, alone or in alliance with OSMs, has been addressed by many within the adult education literature. Fourth, and most important for this study, is the question of the politics of adult education in social movements and civil society—in other words, toward what we are working and educating. As Lovett (1988a) says, "the whole discussion about adult education and social change, about the role of adult education in popular social movements, is intelligible only in relation to the question of purpose" (p. 300).

CAN EDUCATION CHANGE SOCIETY?

The question of whether education can change society is, at first, relatively simple; indeed, there are several examples within the literature of people providing straightforward, negative responses to the question. Paulston and Altenbaugh (1988), for example, in discussing the various forms of adult education in Finnish Labor Colleges and the Black Panther Party, say that "radical adult education is perhaps best understood as radical because of its service to radical movements" (p. 134). In other words, because the education that they noticed within these movements was largely "concerned with teaching basic skills such as literacy or running a co-op or a health center" (p. 134), which could be taught in any context by anyone, they conclude that the education itself was not radical, but the actions of the movements were. Mayo (1993) agrees with Paulston and Altenbaugh. He says that "adult education, no matter how emancipatory in process and content it may be, does not on its own lead to social transformation" (p. 14). Zacharakis-Jutz (1991) takes a similar position and directs the issue to what he sees as the misconceived notion that some people have that adult education is a movement of its own. "Clearly education cannot be a social movement unto itself. Rather, education is an instrument of power which shapes knowledge within social movements" (p. 9). Hall (1978) says that "a political economic view of adult education would not allow for the conclusion that adult education, or in fact any education alone, is an instrumental factor in changing society" (p. 13).

Indeed, it would seem clear, then, that education does not change society. To think that changing perspectives of the world changes the world itself is to fall into the worst form of idealism, which Marx and Engels (1976) rightfully criticized in the opening pages of *The German Ideology*. The question does not simply end there, however, for as Hall (1978) goes on to say, "knowledge is produced and renewed by continuous testing, by acting upon one's theories, by reflecting upon one's actions, and by beginning the cycle again. It is the combination of social transformation and education that has created the kind of knowledge which forges the personal and communal commitment for sustained engagement" (pp. 13–14). Now the question, at a more profound level of analysis, becomes more complex. At this point we realize that perhaps we are asking the wrong question. Now the question is "Can we speak of social change and education as separate?" This is not merely an academic question for it speaks to exactly how we define adult education.

Marx (Marx & Engels, 1976), in his theses on Feuerbach that he wrote in preparing *The German Ideology*, addresses the relationship between education and action when he says, "The materialist doctrine concerning the changing of circumstances and upbringing forgets that circumstances are changed by men and that the educator must himself be educated. . . . The coincidence of the changing of circumstances and of human activity or self-change can be conceived and rationally understood only as *revolutionary practice*" (pp. 615–616). "Revolutionary practice," or praxis, is the dialectical unity of theory (knowledge, speculation of the world, education) and practice (the actions of social movements). We should not and cannot conceive of one without the other. Freire (1984) calls theory without action "verbalism" and action without theory "activism." It is interesting to see the relation of education and social change analyzed by Horton and Freire (1990); Horton consciously separates organizing and education in his thought and practice.

Myles [Horton]: Saul [Alinsky] says that organizing educates. I said that education makes possible organization, but there's a different interest, different emphasis.... We [Highlander] emphasize ways you analyze and perform and relate to people, but that's what I call education, not organizing. (pp. 115–116)

Paulo [Freire]: When we're in the process of mobilizing or organizing, it begins to be seen also as an educational problem.... Education is *before*, is *during* and is *after*....
  What I want to say is that it's impossible to organize without educating and *being* educated by the very process of organizing. (pp. 119–121)

We see in this interchange that Freire captures the dialectic of education and change in praxis. Furthermore, Youngman (1986), Torres (1990), and Foley (1999) all problematize this dialectic by placing education within an overall analysis of the social totality. "Like other institutions of the superstructure, education must also be viewed as an arena of class struggle. While reproducing the capitalist mode of production it also reproduces the contradictions inherent in that mode" (Youngman, 1986, p. 22). This quality of being a site for both reproduction and struggle is the basis for the idea that education is not neutral. While we often credit Freire with this "discovery," it was clearly understood at least as far back as Lenin (1920/1969), who, in speaking to a conference of political education workers, argued that the idea of "apolitical" education was "a piece of bourgeois hypocrisy" (p. 39). It is in this sense that Cunningham (1988) affirmatively answers the question she poses as to whether social change can be accomplished through education with the following qualifier: "To the extent that adult educators can assist individuals in creating, disseminating, legitimating, and celebrating their own knowledge (including cultural knowledge), social change can occur" (p. 137). When we view adult education form this vantage point, it opens up the field to a much wider array of activities, such as the informal educational activities of German immigrants in nineteenth-century Chicago, analyzed by Schied (1993). These informal activities should be seen as educational, and they have been by those who have studied the nature of education within social movements.

THE NATURE OF EDUCATION IN SOCIAL MOVEMENTS

It is recognized in the literature that there has been a general tendency to dismiss the importance and nature of learning in social movements. This reluctance stems from (a) viewing social movement practice as political and not educative; (b) the tendency in adult education to dismiss informal education in everyday life; and (c) the increasing professionalization of the field, which has moved the field away from its historical roots within social movements themselves (Dykstra & Law, 1994).

Nevertheless, there have been attempts to identify the specific types of educational activity that take place in social movements. It is generally recognized (Crowther & Shaw, 1997; Dykstra & Law, 1994; Kastner, 1990; Martin, 1988; Selman, 1990) that there are two targets and corresponding forms of education in social movements. First, social movements, through public protest that can take various forms, attempt to educate and persuade the larger public and politicians. Second, there is much educational work internal to social movements, in which organizational skills, ideology, and lifestyle choices are passed from one member to the next informally through mentoring and modeling or formally through workshops, seminars, lectures, and so forth. In addition, with the emergence of NSMs, theorists influenced by postmodernism (Arvidson & Stenøien, 1997; Bergstedt, 1992; Finger, 1989) have argued that these new movements engage in a fundamentally different and more authentic form of education that centers on personal transformation rather than simply using education to transform society.

As stated at the beginning of this chapter, the debates within adult education over social movements reflect the dichotomy between radical pluralists and socialists in the wider debates over social movements. In this section, we will see how adult educators from these perspectives address the nature of adult education within social movements.

Radical Pluralist Perspectives

Ron Eyerman & Andrew Jamison

Sociologists Ron Eyerman and Andrew Jamison (1991)—who, like many practitioners of adult education, would never identify themselves or their work within adult education—provide a theoretical framework to analyze the relationship between adult education and social movements. They describe their work as an effort to combine critical theory of the Marxist tradition (particularly Habermas) and the sociology of knowledge to analyze what they call the *cognitive praxis* of social movements. By focusing on the cognitive praxis of social movements, they hope to move social theory beyond the impasse of the competition between the major social movement paradigms of RM theory and NSM theory that we saw in Chapter 2. This focus places their analysis squarely within the realm of adult education theory, even though it has largely been ignored in that field (for exceptions see Arvidson & Stenøien, 1997; Crowther & Shaw, 1997; Holford, 1995).

We can see their effort to combine Marxist analysis and Habermas's emphasis on communicative interaction in the following quote, which succinctly summarizes their approach to social movements (Eyerman & Jamison, 1991):

Social movements express shifts in the consciousness of actors as they are articulated in the interactions between activists and their opposition(s) in historically situated political and cultural contexts. The content of this consciousness, what we call cognitive praxis of a movement, is thus socially conditioned. . . . In other words, social movements are the result of an interactional process which centers around the articulation of a collective identity and which occurs within the boundaries of a particular society. Our approach thus focuses upon the process of articulating a movement identity (cognitive praxis), on the actors taking part in this process (movement intellectuals), and on the contexts of articulation (political cultures and institutions). (p. 4)

Cognitive praxis is the most basic of their concepts (p. 44), and "a social movement *is* its cognitive praxis" (p. 54). Following Habermas's conceptualization of human interests, they list three dimensions of cognitive praxis: (a) cosmological, or "basic assumptions or beliefs"; (b) technological, or the "specific topics of . . . protest"; and (c) organizational, or "an ambition to deprofessionalize expertise and develop new, more democratic forms of knowledge production" (p. 66). The production of knowledge is central to the development of collective identities within social movements, and through this process of identity formation, "much if not all new knowledge emanates" (p. 59). In their closest references to adult education, they say that the production of knowledge and collective identity is "a process of social learning" (p. 55) and that they are interested in "formalized and informal modes of knowledge production within social movements" (p. 43). Although they do not discuss the specifics of the learning process, be it formal or informal, they do introduce the concept of *movement intellectual*, adapting Gramsci's concept of *organic intellectual*. "We use the term movement intellectual to refer to those individuals who through their activities articulate the knowledge interests and cognitive identity of social movements. They . . . create their individual role at the same time as they create the movement, as new individual identities and a new collective identity take form in the same interactive process" (p. 98).

Eyerman and Jamison are successful in their goal to "open up new conceptual spaces and provide a set of new assumptions for social analysis" (p. 160) of social movements. As they show in their case study of the civil rights movement in the United States and the comparative study of the environmental movement, their conceptual framework is useful in bringing to the fore the importance of learning and knowledge production within social movements; adult educators interested in social movements need to take this work seriously. For all that Eyerman and Jamison provide, however, there is a fundamental flaw in their analysis that limits its ultimate utility. In their effort to combine critical theory and the sociology of knowledge for an analysis of cognitive praxis, they overemphasize the work of Habermas, which clouds the importance of political economy and an analysis of political praxis. Social movements are more than knowledge producers. As they themselves recognize, "for most social movement activists . . . the cognitive interests and activities of the movements . . . are largely taken for granted" (p. 45). This is not by accident, for as anyone involved in a movement knows, knowledge is a tool for the important work of political praxis. In other words, we change people's minds in order that we may use that knowledge to change the world. We must be careful not to lose sight of the dialectic between education and action embodied in the term *praxis* itself for an overemphasis of action, but, equally, we cannot also overemphasize the cognitive aspect to the detriment of action, which is the case with Eyerman and Jamison.

The problem begins with their idea that "knowledge . . . is a fundamental category, . . . the basis or the working material for . . . *the social construction of reality* [italics added]" (p. 49). Reality is socially constructed to the extent that we create the social world. This construction, our interaction with the material world and with knowledge central to it, is mediated by an independent, existing material reality that has nothing to do with knowledge and is in no way of our making. This is a fundamental premise of materialism; its opposite, the idealist premise that we construct reality with our ideas, makes its way into Eyerman and Jamison's notion of cognitive praxis. Through the use of the term *praxis* in their concept of cognitive praxis, they make an effort to underscore the practical activity involved in the formation of movement identity, but this remains underdeveloped. This is underscored by the fact that the term *political praxis* does not appear until page 62 of the book. It is important to point out, moreover, that they *do* make a distinction between cognitive and political praxis. "Social movements are at once conditioned by the historical contexts . . . and, in turn, affect that context through their cognitive and political praxis" (p. 62). Although they admit that they "do not mean to suggest that the emergence or political influence of . . . any social movement . . . can be explained solely on the basis of its cognitive praxis" (p. 67), they virtually ignore the political for the cognitive, thus leaving themselves open to an overemphasis on the ideal and not the material. The concept of cognitive praxis provides a framework for a theory of adult education in social movements, yet it must be tempered by an analysis of the relationship between cognitive *and* political praxis.

Their dependence on Habermas and critical theory in general also taints their political perspective. They adopt not only an overemphasis of discourse from critical theory but a limiting social democratic political perspective as well. This is most apparent in their case study of the civil rights movement in the United States. That chapter presents a classic social democratic reading of the civil rights movement that sees its destruction at the point of the emergence of the Black Power movement and revolutionary organizations in the North. They even go so far as to flirt with a blame-the-victim type of approach when they discuss how the "extreme left" stance of the post-1965 Student Nonviolent Coordinating Committee (SNCC) and the Black Panther Party could justify government repression of these organizations (p. 138). If they had taken a political economic approach, they would have seen that the more militant stance of later organizations such as SNCC and the League of Revolutionary Black Workers was in many ways a return to the economic issues of poverty and joblessness that were among the central issues of the long history of Black organizing in the South that laid the groundwork for the movement in the 1950s and 1960s. The directly economic issues were often overshadowed in the Southern movement until King took them up again with the Poor People's Campaign.

Eyerman and Jamison's lack of political economy is also evident in their conceptualization of movement intellectuals. They list civil rights activists Martin Luther King Jr., Roy Wilkins, Ralph Abernathy, Robert Moses, and Ella Baker as movement, or organic, intellectuals. All of these very important leaders were college-educated and middle class. The question here is how we apply a class analysis–based terminology (Gramsci's concept of organic intellectuals) to a movement that can be seen as a movement of national liberation or as a movement of a racial group for racial justice. From either perspective, we have interclass alliances and, therefore, can see leaders of the middle class as organic to the movement as a whole. This was not, however, Gramsci's idea of organic intellectuals. By conflating organic intellectuals (Gramsci's concept of class leaders) with movement intellectuals (regardless of class), there is no room to analyze the emergence of working-class African-American leaders who view the struggle of the civil rights movement as part of a struggle for national liberation and/or socialism. This is not just an issue for the civil rights movement of the 1960s. Throughout the long struggle for African-American liberation, there have been leaders emerging who represent distinct classes. So, for example, Booker T. Washington, W.E.B. DuBois, and Harry Haywood (1978) represent different classes among African Americans and therefore align themselves with correspondingly different organizations. Although we can analyze the formation of all of these leaders as movement intellectuals, Gramsci's concept of organic intellectuals forces us to view this formation from a perspective informed specifically by class (see Peery, 1978, pp. 28–57). Gramsci's concept also forces us to take very seriously the educational role of movements in forming organic intellectuals from the working class. Yes, King, Abernathy, Moses, and Baker were essential to the civil rights movement; the movement work they were a central part of—organizing, demonstrating, and educating—produced organic intellectuals from the Black share-croppers and working class throughout the South. These working-class organic intellectuals were the direct result of a radical adult education worthy of further investigation.

For adult educators, this problem is important when we see how Holford (1995), who basically attempts to "translate" Eyerman and Jamison's work into adult education, makes the same mistake, in terms of automatically labeling adult educators as organic intellectuals (see Foley, 1999, Chapter 8, for a critique of Holford).

Although Eyerman and Jamison provide the most comprehensive radical pluralist perspective from outside the field of adult education, others within the field have also approached the nature of social movement education from this perspective.

Radical Pluralist Approaches in Adult Education

As we saw in Chapter 2, fundamental to the radical pluralist perspective is an emphasis on the newness of NSMs. It is argued that the emergence of postindustrial societies marks the birth of qualitatively new social actors with equally unique demands, forms of organization, and relations to knowledge. This, we can see as highlighted in Table 1, is the starting point for Arvidson and Stenøien (1997). "The workers' movement and other 'older movements' appeared at the time of industrialization and are strongly attached to the welfare state. The new social movements attach themselves to the end of the industrial society. We have to ask how their different outlooks on the nature of society influence their views on knowledge and social participation" (p. 216).

The problem with Arvidson and Stenøien's analysis is the problem of radical pluralism in general. The comparisons of Table 1 create a false dichotomy based on the inadequate political economic analysis that I discussed in detail in Chapter 2. The elements listed as specific to either of the two types of movements can be found in both. OSMs, as Eyerman and Jamison (1991) have shown, can also be seen as cognitive praxis; NSMs, such as the civil rights movement in the United States and the peace movement, have created their own educational institutions; NSMs have called for fair distribution of social resources as OSMs have challenged what they rightly see as the unequal distribution of risks such as health and safety issues; and finally, both OSMs and NSMs have advocated and implemented representative and direct forms of democracy. Given the problematic nature of the premises, the analysis of knowledge,

Table 1
Arvidson and Stenøien's Comparison of Old and New Social Movements

Criteria of Comparison	Old Social Movements	New Social Movements
Social outlook	Welfare state	Risk society (Beck)
	Rational outlook for economic growth, expansion, and fair distribution.	Economic growth and expansion create democratically distributed risks (e.g., pollution). Consciousness of risk is through knowledge and, therefore, control of knowledge is key.
Knowledge processes or Knowledge environments	Change is demanded in the formal educational system, and their own educational institutions and forms of education are created.	The movement itself is a form of "cognitive praxis" (Eyerman & Jamison, 1991).
View of democracy	Representative	Direct
	Hierarchical communication between leaders and the represented.	Horizontal relations.

its control, and learning within social movements also become problematic. To argue that "when the risk society develops, . . . the social and economic importance of knowledge increases" (p. 219) simply ignores the history of OSMs and their relationship to knowledge.

Kilgore (1999) provides some preliminary indications of what she calls a *theory of collective learning*. Like Cunningham (1998), she begins by stressing the inadequacies of individualized, psychology-based theories of adult education for understanding adult education that is interested in social justice issues and the power relations inherent in self-directed learning. For Kilgore (1999), "a theory of collective development and learning involves both individual and group components. Individual components . . . are identity, consciousness, sense of agency, sense of worthiness and sense of connectedness. . . . Components of collective development . . . include collective identity, group consciousness, solidarity and organization" (pp. 196–197). While Kilgore correctly states that the individual and the group must be seen as a dialectical totality (p. 197), like Arvidson and Stenøien, her reliance on radical pluralist theory—namely, Melucci—limits the overall utility of her theory. She argues that contemporary social movements "challenge dominant cultural meanings.

. . . Rather than addressing a structural issue like class, these kinds of movements address cultural symbols" (p. 198). Therefore, "collective learning consists mainly of the construction of collective identity" (p. 197). While we can agree that some new social movements do not always directly address class relations, they clearly go beyond cultural symbol formation in their struggles within and against institutions, for reforms, and in electoral politics. Adult educators who base their social analysis on radical pluralist theory are developing theories of education within social movements that address identity and cultural formation, yet their theories will remain inadequate while they fail to problematize relations of power based in political economy (see Foley, 1994).

Socialist Perspectives

Corina Dykstra and Michael Law

Corina Dykstra and Michael Law (1994) provide what they call a pro-visional theoretical framework for understanding social movements as educative forces. Although they recognize the fact that much of what social movements do is obviously educative, such as seminars, work-shops, teach-ins, and distribution of leaflets, they also argue that there is "an equally important sense in which the full life of a social move-ment—poetry, music, petitions, pickets, and so forth—brings culture and politics together in an inherently educative way" (p. 122). Radical plu-ralists (e.g., Welton, 1993) argue that this latter pedagogical aspect is precisely what characterizes the newness of NSMs, yet Dykstra and Law point out that the latter and the former aspects can characterize both OSMs and NSMs (p. 123). (See Figure 1.)

The elements outlined in Figure 1, as we shall see below, are interre-lated. The educational aspect of a social movement's vision lies in the fact that it allows participants to "construct an alternative map of real-ity." Critical pedagogy is the practice of social movements "that critically informs, challenges and engages people in the creation and re-creation of knowledge." Fundamental to critical pedagogy is social consciousness, or the ability to "unmask power relations" and to see how consent to these relations is manufactured (p. 123). It is through critical thinking and experiential learning that people can develop social consciousness within a social movement. Imagination, like the vision of a social move-ment, allows people to transcend the everyday and think of alternatives. Dialogue, for Dykstra and Law, is more than a technique; it is a descrip-tion of relations within social movements and in itself "constitutes a form of resistance to the dominant relations" (p. 124).

The pedagogy of mobilization is the learning inherent in the building and maintaining of a social movement and its organizations. Through

Figure 1
Outline Showing the Educational Elements and Subelements in Dykstra and Law's Framework

I.   Vision
II. Critical pedagogy
     A. Social consciousness
        1. Critical thinking
        2. Experiential learning
     B. Imagination
     C. Dialogue
III. Pedagogy of mobilization
     A. Organizing and building
     B. Continuing participation
        1. Leadership development
        2. Development of analytical and strategic thinking
     C. Political action
     D. Coalition and network building

participation in a social movement, people learn numerous skills and ways of thinking analytically and strategically as they struggle to understand their movement in motion; in this process they move beyond what Gramsci (1971) referred to as common sense. Moreover, as coalitions are formed, people's understanding of the interconnectedness of relations within a social totality become increasingly sophisticated.

Dykstra and Law's framework is, in their own words, provisional; it only provides a framework from which to build. Nevertheless, it has already been shown to be of value for guiding studies of social movement educational practice (Cunningham, 1998, pp. 22–25). Furthermore, even though I have placed their framework within the socialist perspective because I believe it avoids the pitfalls of an overemphasis on identity formation and culture, its political perspective is not explicit. This is not the case with other socialist adult educators, who have specifically addressed the nature of a socialist education within social movements.

Frank Youngman, Paula Allman & John Wallis, and Griff Foley

We can now turn to an analysis of adult educators who write from an explicitly socialist or Marxist perspective. Here we will find work that emphasizes the distinctive nature of an education for socialism in nonformal and informal social movement settings. The writers I mention here do not necessarily write from a common paradigm, yet there are enough similarities in their work to allow me to discuss them together.

Frank Youngman's book *Adult Education and Socialist Pedagogy* was one of the first and most comprehensive efforts to relate Marxist theory to the field of adult education. As Youngman (1986) himself comments, "in the burgeoning literature in English which considers adult education as a field of study, very few authors have taken an explicitly socialist perspective" (p. 3). Youngman begins with the basic Marxist tenet that adult education "must be analyzed within its economic and political context" (p. 15). He then applies this to an analysis of a wide range of issues in adult education: traditional learning theories, Marxist theories of learning, a critique of Freire, the role of political parties, and the politics of adult education in general. What is of most interest to us here, however, is his discussion of the aims and methods of socialist pedagogy.

For Youngman, the aims of socialist adult education are the following: "a) to challenge the ideology and culture of capitalism and create a counter-hegemony; b) to develop the general knowledge and technical expertise necessary to reorganize production and society in a fully democratic way" (p. 197). Therefore, "socialist adult education can be conceptualized in terms of three dimensions—political, general, and technical education. (These should be considered as dimensions of a single activity and not as separate entities)" (p. 198).

Youngman's point (a) above is not unique. Many (Allman, 1988; Allman & Wallis, 1997; Cooper, 1998; Foley, 1999; Hall, 1988; O' Cadiz & Torres, 1994; Reed, 1981) have argued from both radical pluralist and socialist perspectives that central to education within social movements is the challenging of dominant hegemony. What is unique to Youngman is his point (b), in which he insists on general and technical education. In other words, if we are serious about socialism and the working class taking power, then we need to be prepared for precisely that task. The working class needs general and technical knowledge to run society. Marx (1867/1977a), Gramsci (1971), and Guevara (1994), to name just a few in the classical Marxist tradition, all understood, along with Youngman, that this education takes two forms. First—and this point is not new, as we can see it in Dykstra and Law's analysis, among others— socialist struggle is implicitly educative. Through organizing, debating and developing tactics and strategy, confronting institutions of power, and all the multifaceted forms of reflecting and acting, people gain practical skills that prepare them in part for a socialist transformation of society. Second, however, certain skills and knowledge must be taught so that working people can take over and transform the major institutions of society. If through socialist struggle and transformation the working class is to take control of the social, economic, and political institutions, it must acquire vast amounts of technical and scientific knowledge. Only by and through the acquisition of these skills and knowledge can the working class hope to overcome the alienation inherent in capitalist relations. In this educational process, Youngman (1986) insists that "a Marxist approach to adult education advocates an 'explicit curriculum' which seeks to realize in adult education processes socialist values and beliefs and to establish new 'social relations of education' alongside a socialist content" (p. 106).

As I have already mentioned, Youngman's point (a) above ("to challenge the ideology and culture of capitalism and create a counter-hegemony") has been discussed by others. Two people who have moved us the furthest in a Marxist approach to this point are Paula Allman and John Wallis. Specifically, it is through their numerous discussions of dialectics and praxis that they have developed within adult education a Marxist or Gramscian approach to hegemony.

In a comparative analysis of Gramsci and Freire, Allman (1988) shows how Freire's concept of conscientization is a pedagogical articulation of Gramsci's idea of building proletarian hegemony. It is important to note the use of *proletarian hegemony*, because it focuses us precisely on Gramsci's dialectical understanding of the class nature of hegemony. The term *counter-hegemony* does not account for the creative aspect of conscientization: the creation of new knowledge—a working-class outlook that goes beyond countering the bourgeois outlook to creating a fundamentally new way of conceiving the world.

In classical Marxist terminology, Freire's concept of conscientization can be conceived of as revolutionary praxis. Allman and Wallis (1990) remind us that Marx's praxis is directly related to his dialectical understanding of human consciousness. "They [these forms of consciousness] have no history, no development; but [humans], developing their material production and their material intercourse, alter, along with their actual world, also their thinking and the products of their thinking. It is not consciousness that determines life, but life that determines consciousness" (Marx & Engels, cited in Allman & Wallis, 1990, p. 16). Given this dialectical understanding of consciousness, Allman and Wallis argue that "our ... consciousness [and ideas] can only change ... to the degree that we engage in transforming or abolishing the social relations from which they arise" (p. 16). For a revolutionary praxis, then,

we must begin our struggle ... within the problematic mess the current system throws in the face of ourselves and those with whom we work. ... But we also must have some idea of how these phenomena, the surface appearances, relate to the current developments in the dialectic contradictions of capitalism. At the very least we must understand that they do relate, and we must trust that we can re-pose any of these problems as a challenge and then work with others to come to ... a dialectical understanding ... of the causes. (pp. 20–21)

Moreover, they insist that revolutionary praxis requires two fundamental changes in traditional forms of education. First, we must change our relationship to and understanding of knowledge. "Without a thorough grasp of the dialectical nature of our reality, it is likely that our understanding may be at best partial and fragmented. . . . Acknowledging the genesis of knowledge from historically located praxis enables us to recognize forms of understanding as potentially problematic" (p. 21). Second, and echoing Freire (1984), they insist that the teacher-student contradiction must be overcome. "By no means is this a 'technique' of group work; nor is it a crude relativism that claims all perceptions, values and 'myths' have equal value. Without the traditional dialectic of the teacher-student being transformed into conditions where all participants share those roles, then the very act of knowing itself cannot take place" (p. 23). Therefore, a revolutionary praxis is based on a dialectical understanding of the relationship between consciousness and material life and must also be initiated by people who begin with this foundation (Allman & Wallis, 1995a, pp. 18–19). Through educational practice informed by this dialectical relationship that struggles to overcome the student-teacher contradiction, we can begin the process of building working-class hegemony. Obviously, the role of organization, fundamental to Allman and Wallis's analysis, is missing here and will be taken up in the final chapter.

The importance of Griff Foley's contribution to an understanding of socialist pedagogy, or what he calls *learning in the struggle* (1999, p. 39), consists of two main points that at times echo Youngman and Allman and Wallis and at other times depart from them in significant ways. First, Foley (1999) has emphasized the informal nature of much social movement learning. "While systematic education does occur in some social movement sites and actions, learning in such situations is largely informal and often incidental—it is tacit, embedded in action and is often not recognized as learning" (p. 3). Again, this is not an idea unique to Foley, as we have seen it in the work of others mentioned above, and it was recognized in England as *education by collision* at least as far back as the Anti-Corn-Law campaign of the mid-1800s (Dobbs, 1919/1969, Chapter 7). Notwithstanding this long recognition of the phenomenon of incidental learning, it is still, as Foley (1999) states, poorly understood by adult educators (p. 65).

What Foley adds to the discussion of informal learning in social movements, however, can be seen as his second major contribution. He, like Youngman (2000) and Allman (1999), insists upon the fundamental importance of political economy for an understanding of education in social movements (Yarnit, 1995, comes close to Foley in this regard). He is emphatic that "a critique of capitalism must lie at the heart of emancipatory adult education theory and practice" (Foley, 1999, p. 6). Specifically, regarding social movements he argues that "an understanding of the varied and changing ways in which the political economy of capitalism plays itself out in particular situations is central to a strong account of learning in struggle" (p. 66). Following Allman and Wallis and Youngman, Foley believes that "people's everyday experience reproduces ways of thinking and acting which support the, often oppressive, status quo, but . . . this same experience also produces recognitions which enable people to critique and challenge the existing order" (pp. 3–4). Here again the question of hegemony becomes central to an understanding of education and the struggle between the classes for hegemony. Tacit learning, our focus for the moment, is often, like formal schooling, a process of domestication. In other words, we learn the dominant hegemony of the ruling class. The battleground, the social relations within which this "learning" takes place, is always contested territory and is therefore open, in ever-changing degrees, to the creation of alternative hegemonies. Foley's contribution to this discussion is to always bring us back to political economy as the fundamental analytical tool for understanding this battleground in motion.

> The reproduction of capitalism, or any social order, is not a smooth process; it is a continually contested one. . . . The story of this is one of gains and losses, of progress and retreat, and of a growing recognition of the *continually contested, complex, ambiguous and contradictory* nature of the struggle between domination and liberation. . . . Within capitalist modes of production, fundamental contradictions operate in all spheres of social life: in production, in institutional life, and in cultural practices. Examination of contradiction in the arena of cultural practices is of great interest to the study of informal learning in capitalist social formations. (Foley, 1994, p. 129)

Before moving on to an analysis of the politics of social movements and civil society in adult education, I would like by way of summary to enumerate the five major points of the nature of adult education in social movements from a socialist perspective. Because Dykstra and Law provide a framework for the analysis of adult education and not so much a framework for the practice of adult education in social movements, this summary will draw particularly from the work of Youngman, Allman and Wallis, and Foley.

First, adult education practice must be analyzed within its social, political, and economic context. Second, the mode of analysis must be the political economy of the Marxist tradition. Third, education or praxis involves developing a dialectical understanding of the contradictions of social life in order to find avenues of action to overcome the problems facing those with whom we work. This process will inevitably lead to the necessity of confronting and taking power in society; a complementary educational element is the acquisition of the technical and scientific skills and knowledge to make this possible. The development of a dialectical political economic analysis of contradictions and power in capitalist societies, the confrontation of power, and the acquisition of technical and scientific skills in the struggle for power is the development of hegemony. Fourth, this process of critical investigation and action must take the form of a dialogue; this does not negate the fact that leaders will initiate and emerge from the process. Fifth, because we begin with the premise that ideas and beliefs emerge from lived experience (Youngman, 1986, p. 70), the practice of dialogical educational social relations prefigures socialist relations and is essential to the creation of a new hegemony. The nature of this dialogical process of the creation of hegemony and the development of leaders are fundamentally organizational questions that we will examine in the final chapter.

LINKING OLD AND NEW SOCIAL MOVEMENTS

It is quite apparent that where one falls on the radical pluralism–socialist divide largely determines one's position on the question of alliances. There are postmodernist thinkers (e.g., Finger, 1989) who ignore the issue of alliances because they reject OSMs as irrelevant in a postmodern world. Welton (1993), writing from a Habermasian framework, still believes in modernist ideals of emancipation and liberation and feels that NSMs are revitalizing these ideals through their defense of the lifeworld. Because he rejects what he calls the "Leninist dream" of seizing the state and the "Marxist dream" of transforming the economy—two goals of OSMs—he in effect also rejects the relevance of OSMs.

There is a significant socialist perspective in the adult education literature that argues that fundamental social change can come only through an alliance of OSMs and NSMs. Underpinning this perspective is the continuing centrality of class in people's lives (McIlroy, 1995). Alexander (1994) says, "It will be necessary to imaginatively work towards the creation of alliances with and between feminist, anti-racist, ecological and peace movements and with local communities. It is also necessary to broaden the present emphasis on the 'practical' and on 'technicist' solutions in much current education work carried out with and for trade unionists" (p. 38). Field (1988) comments on the displacement of organized labor "from its focal position at the crux of education for social change" (p. 224) in England, whereas Spencer (1995), writing from a Canadian trade-union perspective, challenges the notions that the labor movement (an OSM) is irrelevant as an important site of adult education and that it is oblivious to the demands of NSMs. He argues that "labor unions remain the single most important provider of non-vocational social purpose adult education for working people" (p. 37).

This is particularly important, considering the fact that NSMs operate largely within the middle class. Furthermore, he argues that the "dominant union philosophy in Canada is 'social unionism' " (p. 33), which actively seeks to inject themes of community organizing, environmentalism, and gender and racial equality into the labor movement. Innovative trends of community-labor organizing are again emerging in the United States, particularly among those unions, such as the Service Employees International Union (SEIU) and the Hotel Employees Restaurant Employees (HERE), that deal with largely immigrant workforces. This organizing strategy leads to efforts to link the goals of OSMs and NSMs.

Howlett (1991) and Linds (1991) also see the move toward OSM-NSM coalitions as promising. Howlett, however, insists that we must move beyond mere coalitions. He sees this as both an organizational and an analytical step directly related to the nature of education within social movements. "Challenging people and sectoral social movement organizations to move from a sectoral to a broader structural analysis cannot be done only through content based education or theoretical debates; it requires the development of intersectional personal and organizational relationships of joint analysis and common action. Developing greater class or social consciousness is a key to the struggle for fundamental social transformation" (Howlett, 1991, p. 129).

Whereas Alexander, Spencer, Howlett, and Linds provide general calls to linking OSMs and NSMs, the practical work of Freire in São Paulo, Brazil, and Allman and Wallis's (1995b) critique of the "New Times" project in Great Britain provide concrete examples of strategies for forming alliances.

Torres (1994) discusses Freire's most recent work as secretary of education in the city of São Paulo within the context of the relationship between the Workers' Party (OSM) that won the municipal elections in 1988, São Paulo popular movements (NSMs), and the state. Torres describes the relationship between the Workers' Party administrators in governmental positions, such as Freire, and the social movements as "a partnership between social movements and the municipal state . . . linking human resources from the movements with financial and technical resources from the state" (p. 194). Throughout this process there was significant tension between the social movements and the state. There was a fear among people in the social movements of being co-opted by the state, which in its extreme led to what Freire called *basism*. "There is a kind of illness in the popular politics which we call grassroots movements. But it is not the grassroots movement which is wrong. It is the exacerbation of value of the grassroots movement. Basism means that virtue, knowledge, wisdom, and everything else reside with the masses of the people, the bases, with the grassroots. And those who are not in sight of the grassroots are classified as elites or academics" (Freire, cited in Torres, 1994, p. 209). The problem of basism, which is a form of romanticization of the poor, indicates a weakness in the political strategy of NSMs. NSMs are generally seen, in the literature and in practice, as not interested in taking political power or, more specifically, in seizing hold of the institutions of political power. At what point does a movement move from a defensive strategy to an offensive strategy? Basism is the refusal to make this strategic change when the opportunity is present.

The political strategy of NSMs is at the center of the "New Times" project that Allman and Wallis (1995b) see as a dangerous deviation from the theory and practice of classical Marxism as expounded by Marx and particularly Gramsci. Allman and Wallis argue that the forces of the Communist Party of Great Britain, now called the Democratic Left,

> are not advocating a new form of democracy but simply an expansion of present forms into wider areas of social existence. This can be seen in the various proposals outlined in their "New Times Manifesto." . . . Current tactics . . . are aimed at forging a "counterhegemonic" historical bloc. To accomplish this task great emphasis has been placed on the Party, movement or social group forming alliances with other "progressive" social movements and forces. Often the concept of alliance is used very loosely in that to ally means simply to include other group's agendas within one's own, or to participate enthusiastically in events and spectacles that give vent to popular fears and aspirations. (p. 132)

Allman and Wallis argue that this conceptualization dilutes Gramsci's notion of alliances. They say that "Gramsci was a realist who would consider temporary alliances so long as the primacy of the [working] class objective could be advanced" (p. 133). Gramsci was interested not in counter-hegemony—he never used this term—but in proletarian hegemony. Counter-hegemony, which speaks to a broad coalition of multiclass formations, by necessity derails the proletarian socialist movement away from its anticapitalist project.

> The point is that an authentic party of the left cannot be *based* on "secondary questions" [Gramsci's term for what we would see today as the concerns of new social movements]; however, this does not mean, within Gramsci's Leitmotiv, that these are ignored. Instead they are supported with a true commitment based on the understanding that the entire range of human aspirations, . . . can be realized only through *pro*-active struggle within new, harmonious social relations of production—a communistic social formation. (p. 135)

For Allman and Wallis, the truly immense and educative project of a party of the left is to engage all the possible anticapitalist forces in an analysis of the origins of the various forms of oppression in society.

THE POLITICS OF SOCIAL MOVEMENTS, CIVIL
SOCIETY, AND ADULT EDUCATION

As stated throughout this study, we should understand the *politics of social movements* as the potential of social movements to change society. Moreover, the term refers to the specific nature of that change: Are we referring to reforms to the existing political economic system or the revolutionary transformation of society to a qualitatively new one? Much of what we will see in this section is shaped by the interrelated factors of (a) the ascendancy of neoliberalism, (b) the collapse of most socialist societies, and (c) the idea of globalization. Indeed, the whole debate over social movements and the emergence of the concept of civil society within adult education among radical pluralists and socialists is tempered by a sense of newfound realism in the face of historical defeats, or what I have called the crisis of Marxism. The words of John Field (1995) are indicative of this trend: "I . . . think it necessary, with the collapse of the grand utopias that once formed the shared goals of adult education movements, to investigate the mobilizing potential of small utopias" (p. 31). If one reads the major socialist-inspired texts from England that emerged in the heyday of radical community education (Lovett et al., 1983; Thompson, 1980a, 1983; Youngman, 1986; and even Lovett, 1988c), one is left with a sense of tremendous movement and hope for the potential of radical adult education to be an effective vehicle for fundamental social change. One only then need look at Jane Thompson's (1993) "open letter to whoever's left" to see the damping effects of the ascendancy of the right. This same sense of defeat and need for realism permeates much of Mayo and Thompson's (1995) compilation of contributions from many of the same adult educators who wrote with such hope in her 1980 collection, *Adult Education for a Change*. This move in England to more realistic utopias is exemplary of the same trend in nearly all parts of the world (for a critique of recent trends in the United States, see Ginden & Panitch, 2000). In Latin American adult education the idea of *renovación*—renovating and rethinking the idea of revolutionary politics—is particularly prominent in the work of adult educators associated with the Consejo de Educación de Adultos de América Latina (CEAAL) (Alforja-Cepis et al., 1989; Osorio, 1997; Palma, 1991; Picón, 1996).

This section of the study, like all the previous areas, will employ the radical pluralist–socialist dichotomy in its analysis. It will do this, however, by looking specifically at how adult educators conceptualize civil society and its relationship to social movements and adult education. Separate sections of radical pluralist and socialist perspectives on civil society are not tenable because the literature simply does not have a thorough socialist perspective on civil society. As we shall see, a radical pluralist perspective on civil society is well represented, yet from a socialist perspective we merely have scattered cautionary critiques of the limitations and potential co-optation of civil society, social movements, and NGO-based adult education.

Civil Society and Adult Education

The concept of civil society cannot be understood on its own. It has reemerged in a particular historical political context. The literature on civil society in adult education reflects this fact in very explicit ways. Specifically, the concept of civil society is almost always mentioned in the context of globalization. Moreover, those that use the concept of civil society, almost exclusively from what I consider to be a radical pluralist perspective, operate within the framework of a strong globalization perspective (see Chapter 2). As a thorough socialist perspective on civil society is missing in the literature, so is its usually theoretical companion of a longer globalization perspective.

Globalization in Adult Education Civil Society Perspectives

Let us look at the globalization–civil society connection step by step. First, it is generally agreed upon that we have entered a qualitatively new economic epoch. "The world is currently in transition from one paradigm to another. The dominant paradigm has been that of modernization, and we would suggest that we are shifting to a new paradigm of globalization. This has major implications for our understanding of 'progress' and for notions of civil society, the state, the market and their relationships to one another" (Amutabi et al., 1997, pp. 1–2). Second, faithful to the strong globalization view, the implications for the state and market of this new paradigm are the following: (a) the economy today is clearly operating at a global, multinational level (Hall, 1996); (b) due to the global nature of the economy, the nation-state is no longer the political formation in control of the economy (Cunningham, 1996a, 1998; Korsgaard, 1997); (c) because the nation-state can no longer control the devastation wrought by the economy, adult educators must look to the sphere of civil society (Alexander & Martin, 1995; Jackson, 1995; Osorio, 1995; WEA, 1998; Welton, 1997); (d) the major actors in civil society are social movements and NGOs; (e) given the globalization of the economy, the weakening of the nation-state, and the rise of civil society, we must also begin to think in terms of a global civil society and global NGOs (Hall, 1993, 1997).

Defining Civil Society in Adult Education

Given the importance that adult educators place on civil society, and the concept's long and diverse history (see Chapter 3), one would think that there would be extensive definitions of the concept in the literature, yet this is simply not the case. What we do see quite often is the use of the term without any specific definition at all, or the referencing of definitions of theorists outside adult education: Jarvis (1993) relies heavily on Keane's definition; Bron (1995) uses Gidden's definition; and Cunningham (1998) uses Gramsci's definition. Arguably the most comprehensive effort to define civil society within adult education has come from Welton (1995a), who, like others, bases his definition on work outside adult education—namely, that of Habermas. Since he works from a Habermasian perspective, he places emphasis on the concepts of civil society and what he calls *lifeworld*. "The lifeworld is the realm of inter-subjective interaction and adult learning par excellence. It is within the lifeworld that we learn what life means, what binds us together as human beings and what constitutes an autonomous personality. It is in the lifeworld that we organize our common affairs through non-instrumental forms of communication, even though various traditions provide substance to our meaning perspectives and to our interactions" (p. 5). For Welton, the lifeworld includes civil society and also goes beyond it. "All significant social events and processes are directly or indirectly manifest in the lifeworld, and any adequate understanding of human action must move inside the meanings people give to their actions. . . . The lifeworld is, therefore, always more than the 'institutions of civil society' that we speak of in political discourse" (p. 142).

Hall (1993, 1997), assuming the major tenets of the strong view of globalization, argues that we must begin thinking in terms of a global civil society. Furthermore, he is particularly interested in what he sees as the fundamental role of NGOs in civil society. "The concept of civil society, originally articulated by the Italian Antonio Gramsci, . . . has . . . become more and more used within INGO [international NGO] and NGO circles in all parts of the world. It refers to the totality of institutions and human arrangements such as associations, clubs, family structures, cultural organizations which operated with some degree of autonomy independently of the state" (Hall, 1993, p. 11). For Hall (1997), global civil society refers to "at least two related phenomena. The first phenomen[on] can be understood as the sum-total of local, national or regional civil society structures. . . . A second form of global civil society construction is represented by the proliferation of specifically global forms of civil society [INGOs]" (pp. 66–67). NSMs "interact with global civil society in at least four ways: the strengthening of global civil society; defending civil society; expanding civil society and rendering civil society organizations more inclusive" (pp. 68–69).

The radical pluralist vision of civil society sees a sphere of social life relatively autonomous from the state and the market, although civil society is constantly facing intrusion from these forces. In civil society people interact, creating culture and identity through daily life. Social movements and their accompanying NGOs protect civil society from intrusion from the state and the market. Through this process of protecting civil society, social movements help to democratize civil society, and thereby civil society becomes a place of citizenship. The activities of civil society are often informal and nonformal examples of adult education; therefore, adult education has a major role in creating and maintaining civil society. Because the democratizing efforts of citizenship in civil society are seen as forms of adult education, the "civil societarian perspective" (Welton, 1997, p. 28) is often seen in the United States as restoring the legacy of Lindeman (1921, 1926/1961).

As stated above, there is no comprehensive socialist perspective in the adult education literature on civil society. Youngman (1996b), however, does provide some insight into this area. It is important to point out that he believes that theory—and particularly political economic theory of the relationship among the state, civil society, social movement, NGOs, and adult education—is still in a preliminary phase (pp. 212–216). Nevertheless he provides the following definition based on Gramsci.

Whereas political society is an area of contestation by political parties seeking to gain control of state power, civil society is an area of pluralism in which citizens organize a variety of interest groups. Thus the organizations of civil society include bodies like churches, women's groups, farmers' associations, trade unions, environmental groups, community organizations and employers' organizations. The concept of civil society embraces a dynamic relation between the state and society. For example, the space available for the operation of the organizations of civil society varies according to the nature of the regime. (p. 215)

Youngman, in contrast to the radical pluralist perspective, emphasizes the relationship between civil society and the state, whereby civil society can be a site for ruling-class hegemony. In the radical pluralist perspective, civil society is usually seen as a site occupied almost exclusively by common folks interested only in the good and the just (see Cunningham, 1996b, for an exception). Moreover, Youngman (1996b) questions the autonomy of NGOs from the state and ruling-class hegemony, and he states that "the role of NGOs in adult education requires in-depth analysis to determine their place in the struggle of hegemony" (p. 216).

The Politics of Adult Education in Civil Society

From a radical pluralist perspective, as we saw above, adult education has a large role to play in civil society. The question then becomes "What is the ultimate political purpose of this education?" Alexander and Martin (1995) say that "as adult and community educators, we should be concerned in our work to develop a commitment to a civil society which involves democratic participation, equity and public discussion of fundamental moral and political issues" (p. 85). This answer does not take us very far in understanding the specific political project of the civil societarian perspective. Jarvis (1993) is somewhat more forthright in his political project.

While the market economy can produce sufficient material conditions to establish a just and civilized society, where the majority of people have the right to enjoy welfare, culture, and leisure, the instrumental rationality of the market does not contain the mechanisms required to introduce the structural changes into society that would make this possible.... [Civilized society] concerns the structures and procedures of both the state and civil society operating according to the principles of a moral rationality, and this is an antithesis of the rationality of the market. Hence, the civilizing process will continue more effectively if the state intervenes and ensures that there are certain rules and regulations that govern the competitive market and its outcomes, so that some of its results ... might be made available for all its citizens. (pp. 137–138)

Because Jarvis is operating from Keane's definition of civil society and his state–civil society tug-of-war strategy (see Chapter 3), we understand that Jarvis believes in the efficiency of the market if it is tempered by an activist state pushed by civil society.

Welton's position is of a very similar vein to Jarvis's. In a quite politically revealing article on the state of civil societarian adult education in Canada, Welton (1997) openly admits his shock at the crisis of Canadian liberal democracy confronted with "a new Quebec ... and ... First Nations peoples carving out an ambiguous relationship with English Canada and the new Quebec" (p. 27). For Welton, civil societarian adult education "help[s] tilt *the balance of power* [italics added] away from government, bureaucracies and privately owned corporations, in favor of ... civil society" (p. 36). In probably his most straightforward statement on the political aspirations of adult education in social movements and civil society, Welton (1995a) says the following:

Critical adult educators have as their mandate the initiation of political learning processes that (1) target new political actors for recognition and inclusion within political society (a "politics of inclusion"), (2) aim to influence the "universe of political discourse to accommodate new need-interpretations, new identities, and new norms" (a "politics of influence"), and (3) attempt to create receptors within political institutions and to democratize political society (the "politics of reform" [Cohen & Arato, 1992, p. 526]). Thus ... adult educators would be committed to defending an autonomous and exuberant civil society. (p. 155)

Simply put, then, civil societarian adult education is about a politics of inclusion, influence and reform. As he says, "the revolutionary fantasies of the 1960s must give way to a more chastened and modest utopianism" (1997, p. 28).

Conclusion

I will now enumerate the fragments of a socialist critique of civil societarian adult education that can be drawn from the literature, along with my own critical comments.

The most common critique of the civil societarian perspective is the obvious limitations of many NGOs. Mukasa (1996) is typical: "Grassroots development organizations especially in the South must be analyzed from a dialectical perspective. From the people's perspective, they are expressions of mass discontent and opposition to imperialism and the affirmation of a desire for self-reliance and self-direction. However, in the absence of a clearly thought out people's political strategy, the grassroots organizations are being daily subverted by imperialism and their energies pressed into the service of salvaging imperialism" (pp. 100–101). Martin (1997) provides insight into how the particular political economic context of NGOs forces them into fragmented, politically limited projects. "Financing systems which operate through several international co-operation agencies have pushed NGOs into competing for funds and avoiding joint projects. Thus, . . . NGOs are inclined towards partial efforts concentrated unilaterally on different aspects of the same rich popular experience" (pp. 43–44).

Many critics of the civil societarian perspective are troubled by the fact that neoliberals are as enthusiastic about civil society as the radical pluralists are. As the neoliberals enthuse over civil society and grassroots empowerment in order to roll back the social welfare responsibilities of the state, professional adult educators are enthusing over the possibility of receiving funding for grassroots initiatives that amount to the privatization of government services. "International organizations [INGOs] have incorporated into their models the collective subject, the expressions of organized civic society. . . . The crisis of the old model of *Welfare State* is certainly an accomplice in this rediscovery. The strategy that gives it life is influenced by the desire to unload onto society the costs of structural reform and the reduction of the role of the state in the field of education" (Federighi, 1997, p. 12). Manicom and Walters (1997) question the co-optation of adult education vocabulary and hint at the fact that the problem is of a theoretical nature: "The presently favored phrases of aid politics—'strong civil society' and 'capacity building'— are deployed equally by the international financial institutions, the UN family of organizations and the international and national NGOs. How do we distinguish between the empowerment of women as authored by the World Bank and the empowerment of poor women through a popular education process? It is clearly time for some rethinking, realignment and perhaps reaffirmation of the radical tradition" (p. 72).

The critique of NGOs is expanded to social movements by Youngman and Allman and Wallis. Youngman (1996a) is skeptical as to "whether the politics of social movements can defeat the logic of capital, in order to transform the relations of production and thus establish the conditions for building a new social order" (p. 26). Allman and Wallis (1997), rescuing Gramsci from radical pluralist interpretations, attempt to show how loose coalitions of social movements are not what Gramsci had in mind when he spoke of a historical bloc in civil society. "The crucial element for Gramsci in holding social movements together was the 'cement' of ideology, i.e., the analysis of origin of ideas, and in his case the 'philosophy of praxis'.... Without such theoretical/analytical principles, elements within every social movement only cohere—to borrow Marx's term—like 'potatoes in a sack' " (p. 118).

Manicom and Walters' suggestion of the reaffirmation of the radical tradition is fundamental to the future of an adult education interested in a qualitative transformation of society. Notwithstanding Martin's analysis of structural constraints of social movement NGOs, a fundamental problem is a lack of theoretical clarity. Adult educators' aversion to theory is long-standing and recognized by many in the field (Cervero, 1991; Darkenwald & Merriam, 1982; Thompson, 1980b; Welton 1995b). Fundamental to the politics of adult education and social movements is a theory of state-society relations (Torres, 1990; Youngman, 1996a). Radical pluralist adult educators are increasingly looking to Gramsci for insight into the politics and nature of adult education in social movements and civil society. Their approaches to Gramsci, however, often isolate his ideas on civil society from the rest of his theoretical and practical work. If we are to take Gramsci seriously, then we must view his concepts, such as civil society, within the overall trajectory of his political project. It is precisely to this task that I will now turn as a way of concluding this study.

5

Gramsci's Concept of Civil Society Revisited: Implications for a Reconceptualization of Radical Adult Education Theory and Practice

The growing influence of the work of Antonio Gramsci within radical adult education can be seen as part and parcel of the emphasis on civil society and social movements. The concern of this chapter is the way in which many in the field read and interpret Gramsci. Gramsci (1971) himself, in detailing a methodology for studying the work of one of the founders of the philosophy of praxis (Marx), made the following observation: "Search for the *Leitmotiv*, for the rhythm of the thought as it develops, should be more important than that for single casual affirmations and isolated aphorisms" (pp. 383–384). Unfortunately, many radical pluralists simply provide a narrow reading of Gramsci in which his concept of civil society is dealt with in isolation, ignoring the leitmotiv of his work.

Narrow readings of Gramsci that seek theoretical justification for reform-oriented, counter-hegemonic practice in what is identified as civil society are not unique to adult education but permeate the left as a whole. Among both radical pluralists and neo-Marxists, there is an effort to pull Gramsci from his classical Marxist roots and pose him as fundamentally distinct from Marx and, especially, Lenin. For example, writing from a neo-Marxist position, Albert & Hahnel (1978) place Gramsci within a group that they call *unorthodox Marxists*, "not because they were immune to the sway of orthodox notions, but because even *immersed in orthodox waves* [italics added] they have established many new ideas and the heritage we now seek to extend" (p. 13). Here we see an "even though he was orthodox, he really wasn't" argument, which merely distorts the legacy of Gramsci.

Lenin (1943) witnessed this very same phenomenon occurring with the works of Marx, and he had no illusions as to its purpose:

What is happening to Marx's doctrine has, in the course of history, often happened to the doctrines of other revolutionary thinkers and leaders of oppressed classes struggling for emancipation. . . . After their death, attempts are made to turn them into harmless icons, canonize them, . . . at the same time emasculating and vulgarizing the *real essence* of their revolutionary theories and blunting their revolutionary edge. . . . They omit, obliterate, and distort the revolutionary side of its teaching, its revolutionary soul. They push to the foreground and extol what is, or seems, acceptable to the bourgeoisie. All the social-chauvinists are now "Marxists"—joking aside! (p. 7)

This blunting of the revolutionary edge of Gramsci is most evident in the literature on social movements and civil society.

Fundamentally, the problem with radical pluralist advocates of social movements is that they want it both ways. They want to be able to claim the historical legacy and tradition of Marxism (classical) while rejecting its most important elements. They seem to be unable or unwilling to place themselves within their true tradition, social democracy. Bernstein and the utopian socialists should be the historical theoretical figures of contemporary radical pluralists, but the problem is that these figures were severely and rightfully discredited by Marx and Engels and by Lenin and Luxemburg, respectively. Therefore, the radical pluralists, those advocating social movements as the heirs to Gramsci's political party, want to pick and choose from theoretical systems that become meaningless without their constituent elements.

This chapter, then, is an effort to reconceptualize the relationship of Gramsci's notion of civil society with other major aspects of his thought in order to capture the meaning of his use of the term *civil society* within the leitmotiv of his overall thought. Allman and Wallis (1995b) have already set the stage for such an analysis by insisting on Gramsci's firm foundation in Marx's work. They feel that resituating Gramsci's work within Marx is important because the *social amnesia*, as they call it, of contemporary applications of Gramsci "has produced the very type of political projects against which [Gramsci] clearly and consistently argued" (p. 120).

My analysis will place Gramsci's concept of civil society within a broader framework that includes his ideas on the state, the political party and organic intellectuals, spontaneity, hegemony, and alliances. In the conclusion I will discuss the implications of this resituating of Gramsci for radical adult education theory and practice.

THE STATE AND CIVIL SOCIETY

Although I outlined Gramsci's idea of civil society in Chapter 3, a brief review of his conceptualization is necessary at this point, as is a further elaboration of how he viewed the relationship between civil society and the state. In Chapter 3, I emphasized how Gramsci saw civil society as part of the state. This argument runs counter to civil societarian perspectives that argue from a "Gramscian" perspective that civil society is an area relatively independent of the state.

It is important to recall that Gramsci's use of the term *civil society* is part of what he himself recognized as a much larger study of intellectuals and hegemony. Moreover, in early letters from prison, he places the study of intellectuals first on lists he made as preparatory work before beginning his notebooks (Cammett, 1967, p. 189). It is worthwhile to revisit the extract from the letter in which he places his use of the term *civil society* in his study of intellectuals.

The research I have done on the intellectuals is very broad.... My study also leads to certain definitions of the concept of the State, that is usually understood as political Society (or dictatorship, or coercive apparatus meant to mold the popular mass in accordance with the type of production and economy at a given moment) and not as a balance between the political Society and civil Society (or the hegemony of a social group over the entire national society, exercised through the so-called private organizations, such as the Church, the unions, the schools, etc.), and it is within the civil society that intellectuals operate. (Gramsci, 1994a, pp. 66–67)

Here we see Gramsci clearly arguing that civil society should be seen as the "hegemonic" aspect of the state balancing the coercive aspect. This would seem to correspond to Gramsci's further elaborations on the state when he says (1971) "that by 'State' should be understood not only the apparatus of government but also the 'private' apparatus of 'hegemony' or civil society." Gramsci then reiterates the notion of civil society as part of the state by saying that "hegemony over its historical development belongs to private forces, to civil society—which is 'State' too, indeed is the State itself" (p. 261). Finally, Gramsci most clearly proposes an alternative view to the state being separate from civil society when he gives the following equation: "State = political society + civil society, in other words hegemony protected by the armor of coercion" (p. 263).

To be fair, there is some, if very little, textual evidence for those who wish to argue that Gramsci identified civil society as autonomous from the state. In a much-quoted section of the *Prison Notebooks*, Gramsci (1971) describes "two major superstructural 'levels': the one that can be called 'civil society,' that is the ensemble of organisms commonly called 'private,' and that of 'political society' or 'the State'" (p. 12). Here we have a one-sentence indication of Gramsci making a separation between state and civil society, although he locates both in the superstructure that for Marxism has always been the domain of the state in the hands of the ruling class.

The overwhelming evidence, then, would indicate that Gramsci saw civil society as part of the state, and this would conform to his original intent of attempting to understand the role of intellectuals in creating hegemony or consent to the dictates of the ruling group of a given epoch.

Another fundamental question posed by interpretations of Gramsci, particularly by civil societarian adult educators, is the building of civil society. To understand Gramsci's idea of civil society it must be made clear that, unlike the radical pluralists or civil societarians that we discussed in Chapter 4, Gramsci did not advocate building or protecting the existing civil society. For Gramsci, as we saw above, *civil society* was a sociological term used to describe a particular aspect of the state. Although civil society was contested terrain, it was, after all—in the words of Hegel and Marx, from whom he drew the term—*bürgerliche gesellschaft* (bourgeois society), and Gramsci clearly identified civil society as an area in which the ruling class exerts its hegemony over society (for an interesting treatment of the question of translations of *civil society*, see Rehmann, 1999). The struggle for Gramsci, then, was not to build civil society but to build proletarian hegemony.

One can find in the *Prison Notebooks* instances where Gramsci appears to be advocating the idea of building civil society, but these citations must be seen in the context of the general theme Gramsci is treating. For example, in a section titled "Statolatry," Gramsci uses the terms *construct* and *creation of* in reference to civil society. It is worth quoting this section at length in order to see the context in which Gramsci (1971) uses these terms.

Attitude of each particular social group towards *its own State* [italics added]. . . . The term "statolatry" is applied to a particular attitude towards the "government by functionaries" or political society, which in everyday language is the form of State life to which the term of State is applied. . . . The assertion that the State can be identified with individuals . . . , as an element of active culture (i.e., as a movement to create a new civilization, a new type of man and of citizen), must serve to determine the will to construct within the husk of political society a complex and well-articulated civil society, in which the individual can govern himself without his self-government thereby entering into conflict with political society—but rather becoming its normal continuation, its organic complement. For some social groups, which before their ascent to autonomous State life have not had a long independent period of cultural and moral development on their own . . . , a period of statolatry is necessary and indeed opportune. This "statolatry" is nothing other than the normal form of "State Life," or at least of initiation to autonomous State life and to the creation of a "civil society" which it was not historically possible to create before the ascent to independent State life. However, this kind of "statolatry" must not be . . . conceived of as "perpetual." (p. 268)

It is essential to understand that here Gramsci is talking about the phase of the dictatorship of the proletariat after the seizure of state power. Statolatry, as he says, is associated with political society or the commonly understood activity of the state—the coercive aspect. The role that Gramsci attaches to civil society here in a postrevolutionary situation is the noncoercive activity of creating proletarian hegemony or consent to the new order in which "the individual can govern himself" without coming into conflict with political society or the coercive aspect of the state. For the working class, a class without a long "independent period of cultural and moral development," a period of statolatry or dictatorship of the proletariat is necessary because the working class is incapable of sufficiently raising its cultural and moral development without the use of state power. Of course, Gramsci then warns against the dictatorship of the proletariat becoming "perpetual" and preventing the development of "spontaneous" state life within individuals. Therefore, when Gramsci does speak of building civil society, it is within the framework of the dictatorship of the proletariat and the solidification of proletarian hegemony or consent to the new order. This is strikingly similar to Lenin's notion of the dictatorship of the proletariat and the withering of the state outlined in *State and Revolution*, which Gramsci had read by the middle of 1920 (see Davidson, 1977, p. 165). From this analysis, then, it should be clear that Gramsci is not, like civil societarians, advocating the building or protecting of the existing bourgeois civil society, but the continuing creation of proletarian hegemony in a postrevolutionary situation.

In this context the example of contemporary Cuba provides insight into the meaning of building civil society in a post-revolutionary situation. In recent years, Cuba has entered into a rigorous debate over the nature of Cuban civil society and the utility of the concept for the construction of socialism in Cuba (e.g., "Sociedad Civil en Debate," 1999). It is clear that this debate in Cuba is qualitatively distinct from the radical pluralist project I have outlined in this text. David (2000) puts Cuban civil society in the following post-revolutionary context:

It is understandable, then, that this process [post-1959] is characterized from its very beginning for laying the *groundwork for a civil society of a new nature, for a historically new type of political society and state as well as new relations between all of these.* . . . For the first time in the history of the country the cardinal and strategic interests of the traditionally exploited and oppressed masses became the guiding core of institutional . . . politics. . . . In this sense, then, *the revolutionary state is filled with civility and civil society shows through in the state.* (p. 54, my translation)

The Cuban debate on civil society centers on increasing mass political participation. For Gerardo Trueba González (in Ayúz, et al., 2000), the concept of civil society "can be very useful in filling the void accumulated over a long period in the study of the individual-state contradiction in the construction of socialism, starting from our own historical experience. In this sense it can enrich our notions about the political system we defend and make, in this way, an effective contribution to its improvement" (p. 10, my translation).

Therefore, in post-revolutionary situations, one can speak of building civil society, as Gramsci does, and be articulating a political project qualitatively different from civil societarian perspectives promoted in capitalist countries. Simply put, building socialist civil society and capitalist civil society are wholly distinct projects.

Within this framework of understanding, it becomes clear that one cannot simply extract Gramsci's notion of civil society from the place it holds in his overall theoretical and practical project. Indeed, it is widely argued (Bellamy & Schecter, 1993; Bobbio, 1979; Sassoon, 1987; Texier, 1979) that in order to understand Gramsci's concept of civil society, one must also look to his analysis of hegemony, intellectuals, and the state. Furthermore, in order to understand Gramsci's concept of political change associated with civil society, which is the main reason adult educators ultimately look to Gramsci, one must look at his work on alliances, spontaneity, and the political party.

THE POLITICAL PARTY AND ORGANIC INTELLECTUALS

We have seen how Gramsci's concept of civil society was part of his analysis of hegemonic consent of the masses to the ruling class. In this sense hegemony is bourgeois hegemony and one-sided. This, however, was not the only way in which Gramsci used the idea of hegemony. As we saw in Chapter 3, Gramsci also talked of proletarian hegemony, developed through the activities of organic intellectuals in a political party.

How did Gramsci (1971) envision the role of organic intellectuals?

Critical self-consciousness means, historically and politically, the creation of an *elite* of intellectuals. A human mass does not "distinguish" itself, does not become independent in its own right without, in the widest sense, organizing itself; and there is no organization without intellectuals, that is without organizers and leaders, in other words, without the theoretical aspect of the theory-practice nexus being distinguished concretely by the existence of a group of people *'specialized'* [italics added] in conceptual and philosophical elaboration of ideas. (p. 334)

Furthermore, it was precisely the role of the party to foster the development of this elite of specialized organic intellectuals from the working class and to link these organic intellectuals with traditional intellectuals of the middle and upper classes who have adopted revolutionary ideology. "The political party for some social groups [read: classes] is nothing other than their specific way of elaborating their own category of organic intellectuals" (p. 15), and "an intellectual [traditional] who joins the political party of a particular social group is merged with the organic intellectuals of the group itself, and is linked tightly with the group" (p. 16).

Gramsci's concept of the party and its role in forming organic intellectuals who act as a vanguard are strikingly similar to the ideas of Lenin. In fact, Gramsci, endorsed Lenin's framework for the party most forthrightly in an article entitled "The Party Grows in Strength by Combating Anti-Leninist Deviations." "According to Leninist doctrine, the Communist Party is the vanguard of the proletariat: in other words, the most advanced section of a particular class and only of that class. Naturally, other social elements may enter the Party as well (intellectuals and peasants), but that does not alter the fact that the Communist Party is an organic part of the proletariat" (Gramsci, 1994b, p. 269). In this article he also clarifies the importance of traditional intellectuals to the party and the working class when he states that "intellectuals are necessary, then, in the construction of socialism. They have served, as representatives of political science and technology, to give the proletariat a consciousness of its historic mission" (p. 270).

Gramsci (1971) also felt that the role of a working-class political party, made up of mainly working-class organic intellectuals, was to bring socialist consciousness to the vast majority of the working class. "But innovation cannot come from the mass, at least at the beginning, except through the mediation of an *elite* for whom the conception implicit in human activity has already become to a certain degree a coherent and systematic ever-present awareness and a precise and decisive will" (p. 335). Less cryptically, Gramsci (1994b) states, "How does the working class acquire [socialist] consciousness? Marxism affirms and demonstrates, in opposition to syndicalism, that this does not happen spontaneously, but only because the representatives of political science and industrial technology . . . construct a proletarian political science [scientific socialism]. . . . Intellectuals . . . give the proletariat a consciousness of its historic mission" (p. 270).

For Gramsci, the creation of proletarian hegemony is the work of organic intellectuals. Organic intellectuals are not born, but are formed through the educational activities of working-class parties. In the party, organic intellectuals meld with traditional intellectuals who have committed class suicide and work to form a proletarian outlook or consciousness based on the knowledge production of the working class within the perspective of a "proletarian political science."

THE LIMITS OF SPONTANEITY

The idea of socialist consciousness being "given" to the proletariat in the thought of Gramsci, as we see in the last quote of the previous section, is based on his critique of the limits of spontaneity and the economic struggle of the working class. "Trade unions have thus shown themselves to be incapable of overthrowing capitalist society, acting within their own sphere and with their own methods. Union action is incapable of bringing about the emancipation of the proletariat, of leading the proletariat towards that exalted and universal end that it had originally proposed" (Gramsci, 1994b, p. 123). Gramsci believed that educational work within a political party was essential for the creation of organic intellectuals and for moving beyond the limits of spontaneity. The Turin movement was accused by elements within the Italian Socialist Party of glorifying spontaneity. In his address of these charges, we can see how Gramsci (1971) viewed the role of education and the party in pushing beyond the limits of spontaneity.

This element of "spontaneity" was not neglected and even less despised. It was *educated*, directed, purged of extraneous contaminations; the aim was to bring it into line with modern theory [Marxism]—but in a living and historically effective manner. . . . It gave the masses a "theoretical" consciousness of being creators of *historical* and institutional *values*, of being founders of a State. This unity between "spontaneity" and "conscious leadership" or "discipline" is precisely the real political action of the subaltern classes, in so far as this is mass politics and not merely an adventure by groups claiming to represent the masses. (p. 198)

Gramsci did not glorify the spontaneous rebelliousness of the working class. He consistently advocated the necessity of the party to educate this spontaneity, to give it a consciousness of its historic potential. Like Freire (1993, pp. 130–131) he saw the feebleness and inherent reactionary quality of a politics of basism that automatically views the masses as the repository of "truth and virtue."

HEGEMONY

Gramsci's critique of the limits of the spontaneous economic struggle was tied to his analysis of hegemony. We can see the origins of Gramsci's conceptualization of civil society as the area of bourgeois hegemony in his unfinished manuscript on the southern question, which he was working on at the time of his arrest in 1926. In this article, among other issues, he provides an analysis of the problem of hegemony for the working-class movement in the north of Italy. "The first problem to be solved, for the Turin Communists, was that of modifying the political orientation and general ideology of the proletariat itself, as a national element which lives inside the complex of the life of the State and undergoes unconsciously the influence of the schools, of the newspapers, of the bourgeois tradition. It is well known what ideology is propagated through the multifarious forms of bourgeois propaganda among the masses of the North" (Gramsci, 1957, p. 31). In the *Prison Notebooks* he specifically sets out the task of returning to this question of hegemony and, as we know, will go on to apply the concept of civil society to what in 1926 he calls the "complex of the life of the State."

Gramsci believed that only through a political party could the working class overcome bourgeois hegemony. The struggle for power is long and arduous. Gramsci (1971) called this a *war of position*, in which the working class must engage in "long ideological and political preparation, organically devised in advance to reawaken popular passions and enable them to be concentrated and brought simultaneously to detonation point" (p. 110). The ultimate aim for Gramsci (1994b) in the war of position was the creation of proletarian hegemony and sufficient forces to launch an assault on the state. "The Turin communists had raised, in concrete terms, the question of the 'hegemony of the proletariat': in other words, the question of the social basis of the proletarian dictatorship and the workers' State. For the proletariat to become the ruling, the dominant, class, it must succeed in creating a system of class alliances which allow it to mobilize the majority of the working population against capitalism and the bourgeois State" (p. 316). Fundamental to the creation of proletarian hegemony is what we can call organs of people's power; for Gramsci these were the factory councils like the Soviets in Russia. These are the organizational form of the workers' state—the dictatorship of the proletariat—created by and for the working class, that can wield political power and create a new economic formation.

THE IMPORTANCE OF ALLIANCES

As we can see in the last quote above, Gramsci argued that class alliances were fundamental for the working class's struggle for power. "Although every party is the expression of a social group [class], and of one social group only, nevertheless in certain given conditions certain parties represent a single social group precisely in so far as they exercise a balancing and arbitrating function between the interests of their group and those of other groups, and succeed in securing the development of the group which they represent with the consent and assistance of the allied groups" (Gramsci, 1971, p. 148). Moreover, in reference to the concrete situation of the Communist Party in Italy, Gramsci (1957) says that "the proletariat can become the leading and ruling class to the extent to which it succeeds in creating a system of class alliances" (p. 30).

It is fundamental to understand that Gramsci believed that within the alliance it was essential that the party maintain hegemony; that the party not allow the other alliance forces to steer the movement into reformism or economism. He felt that only a party of specialists (workers and intellectuals) could successfully form an alliance under these conditions. From an educational standpoint, alliances are fundamental for the creation of class consciousness. It is through the direct contact with organic intellectuals of other classes in alliance that the working class can begin to understand capitalism as a whole. Moreover, cross-class alliances move the working class beyond the economic struggle to a position where it can begin to see the political aspects of its struggle—the role of the state and its importance as a target in the struggle for power. Dykstra and Law (1994) make this point in their emphasis of coalitions and networks in their framework, outlined in Figure 1 in Chapter 4.

CONCLUSION

As we can see from the above summary of Gramsci's ideas, his political project is much larger than simply an analysis of civil society. Moreover, the role of a political party is central to his ideas of hegemony, intellectuals, spontaneity, and alliances. Should we, as post-1989 radical adult educators, dismiss this political formation as a historical relic? I believe that this is the gravest of mistakes. What attracts many of us to Gramsci is his notion of the need for organization and alliance, often referred to as the *historical bloc*. We are faced with a historical conjuncture that provides us with social movements as the only major visible manifestation of resistance to the status quo. Those who advocate the need to work in and theorize about these movements admit that they are problematic because they are often temporary and focused on only one aspect of capitalist oppression. Gramsci realized that a stable, disciplined, and permanent organization of specialists (both working-class and intellectuals) was necessary to mold these movements into a protracted, all-encompassing assault upon the state and the capitalist class. The party is a form of organization that can perform this and maintain itself under the repressive conditions that such a struggle would provoke. To think that it can be done in other ways is to ignore the history of twentieth-century revolutionary struggle. One would be hard-pressed to name a revolutionary movement of the twentieth century that did not have parties as major forces within it.

Unfortunately, in the radical adult education literature on Gramsci (Armstrong, 1988; Coben, 1995; Entwistle, 1979; Mayo, 1994a, 1994b), with a few exceptions (Allman & Wallis, 1995b; Morgan, 1987), the fundamental importance that Gramsci gave to the party as an educational and organizational entity is virtually ignored. I have emphasized the place of the party in Gramsci's thought precisely because it is so often ignored. Gramsci's membership in and insistence upon the party was not a historical curiosity of early twentieth-century Marxism that can be merely overlooked; it is one of his most important legacies that we can learn from today.

A theory and practice of revolutionary or radical adult education must explore the pedagogical nature of the most widely adopted and successful form of revolutionary organization of the twentieth century. One could make the case that, in the twentieth century, more radical adult education took place in revolutionary parties than in any other forum, yet the literature, with few exceptions (e.g., Foley, 1993; Umar, 1993), has virtually ignored the educational role of revolutionary parties while trumpeting Gramsci—one of the twentieth century's most vocal advocates for the necessity of a revolutionary party precisely for its educative role.

As a Marxist, Gramsci realized the objective historical role of the working class as a revolutionary class. In other words, the working class, because of its location in the relations of production, was best situated to abolish capitalism. Subjectively, however, Gramsci (1971) realized that the working class does not spontaneously come to an understanding of its social location or potential as a revolutionary class. "The active man-in-the-mass has a practical activity, but has no clear theoretical consciousness of his practical activity, which nonetheless involves understanding the world in so far as it transforms it" (p. 333). In Marxist-Hegelian terms, how does a class move from a class in itself (constituted as an objective class by the relations of production) to a class for itself (a subjective understanding of its position in production and its political mission)? Lenin answered this question by arguing that "through *agitation*, that is political explanation given, not abstractly, but to workers actually experiencing and confronting in action a problem" (cited in Wolpe, 1970, p. 268), the working class would become a class for itself. This political explanation of concrete problems in struggle is radical adult education. This is what Freire emphasized by using the words of Mao Ze-dong: "We must teach the masses clearly what we have received from them confusedly" (cited in Freire, 1984, p. 82). Gramsci also believed that the revolutionary party's role was to be a place of political explanation and education for both masses and leaders. Furthermore,

only when this organic and co-educative relationship was established
between leaders and masses did the philosophy of praxis come alive.

With the extension of mass parties and their organic coalescence with the intimate (economic-productive) life of the masses themselves, the process whereby
popular feeling is standardized ceases to be mechanical and casual . . . and becomes conscious and critical. Knowledge and a judgement of the importance of
this feeling on the part of the leaders is no longer the product of hunches backed
up by the identification of statistical laws, which leaders then translate into ideas
and words-as-force. . . . Rather it is acquired by the collective organism through
"active and conscious co-participation," through "compassionality," through experience of immediate particulars, through a system which one could call "living
philology." In this way a close link is formed between great mass, party and
leading group, and the whole complex, thus articulated can move together as
"collective-man." (Gramsci, 1971, p. 429)

This is why Gramsci (1971) said that "parties can be considered as
schools" (p. 268). For Gramsci, the revolutionary party is an agent of
radical adult education without which there can be no formation of leaders nor proletarian hegemony (p. 227). "One can say that the parties are
the elaborators of new integral and totalitarian [read: all-encompassing]
intelligentsias and the crucibles where the unification of theory and practice, understood as a real historical process, takes place" (p. 335).

   Clearly, then, for Gramsci, adult education within political parties is
central to his overall political project. Adult education in the party—the
process by which the working class theoretically understands its practice,
both economic and political (praxis)—links the masses and leaders in a
co-educative relationship, creates new leaders, forges proletarian hegemony, and overcomes the limits of spontaneity.

   Contemporary radical adult education must reassess its preference for
NSMs over OSMs. Advocates (Carroll & Ratner, 1994; Epstein, 1990; Fuentes & Frank, 1989) of NSMs admit to their limited political potential
due to the fact that they tend to be temporary, middle-class-based, and
easily co-opted into reformism by capitalist democracy, and therefore
they look to Gramsci's concepts of hegemony and historical bloc or alliances to address these shortcomings (Alexander, 1994; Spencer, 1995).
Allman and Wallis (1995b) caution us quite correctly, however, that these
calls for alliances are often "not advocating a new form of democracy
but simply an expansion of present forms into wider areas of social existence" (p. 132). This building or expanding of civil society is not socialism. We must keep in mind Nzimande and Sikhosana's (1995b)
admonition that the struggle for socialism is not "simply an incremental
building upon liberal bourgeois freedoms" (p. 37).

   Maintaining ever-present in our theory and practice the importance
that Gramsci placed on the educative and practical role of the revolu-

tionary party allows us to begin to overcome the politically limiting nature of NSMs. Emphasizing Gramsci's advocation of the revolutionary party is not to say that we must mechanically replicate a monolithic organizational form from the past to all future situations; successful revolutionaries have never done this (e.g., Heagerty & Peery, 2000). If we are, however, to seriously look to Gramsci for insight into the role of adult education in creating and sustaining radical political practice, then we must confront his insistence on the revolutionary party. The building of a revolutionary party was, after all, his life's work.

Gramsci's work, both his theory and practice, looms large over all aspects of the questions posed to adult educators by social movements. Whether it is the question of the role of education in social change, the nature of the educational process within social movements, or the strategy and tactics of social change itself, Gramsci has much to offer those of us interested in furthering our understanding of these questions. Education must be seen as an integral part of the process of social change because our practice informs us that it is so. It is also clear from our practice that the relationship between education and social change must be conceptualized dialectically. The impulse by academics to leave the university and enter the "field" speaks to this very issue, and academics, researchers of the history of our own practice and theory, can make great contributions to social movements. Gramsci's studies on intellectuals, which encompass his analysis of hegemony and civil society, provide vast amounts of material for the further development of theories of radical adult education that are far from complete. Gramsci's ideas on the party and alliances offer enormous potential for developing a theory and practice of uniting NSMs and OSMs. We must be careful, however, to view Gramsci not as we would like him to be but as he actually was, if we are to understand the essence of his ideas.

The historical juncture in which we find ourselves seems to leave us with few options for radical adult education theory and practice, yet we must, as Gramsci did, think dialectically. The subjective impossibility of great historic change that confronts us for the moment merely speaks to the continuing formation of the objective conditions for change of historic proportions.

References

Adam, B. D. (1993). Post-Marxism and the new social movements. *Canadian Review of Sociology & Anthropology, 30* (3), 316–336.

Albert, M., & Hahnel R. (1978). *Unorthodox Marxism.* Boston: South End Press.

Alexander, D. (1994). The education of adults in Scotland: Democracy and curriculum. *Studies in the Education of Adults, 26* (1), 31–49.

Alexander, D., & Martin, I. (1995). Competence, curriculum and democracy. In M. Mayo & J. Thompson (Eds.), *Adult learning, critical intelligence and social change* (pp. 82–96). Leicester, England: NIACE.

Alforja-Cepis, Ghiso, A., Leis, R., Mejía, M. R., Ormeño, E., Osorio, J., & Tapia, G. (1989). *La formación metodológica de los educadores populares* [The methodological preparation of popular educators]. Santiago, Chile: CEAAL.

Allman, P. (1988). Gramsci, Freire and Illich: Their contributions to education for socialism. In T. Lovett (Ed.), *Radical approaches to adult education: A reader* (pp. 85–113). London: Routledge.

Allman, P. (1999). *Revolutionary social transformation.* Westport, CT: Bergin & Garvey.

Allman, P., & Wallis, J. (1990). Praxis: Implications for 'really' radical education. *Studies in the Education of Adults, 22* (1), 14–30.

Allman, P., & Wallis, J. (1995a). Challenging the postmodern condition: Radical adult education for critical intelligence. In M. Mayo & J. Thompson (Eds.), *Adult learning, critical intelligence and social change* (pp. 18–33). Leicester, England: NIACE.

Allman, P., & Wallis, J. (1995b). Gramsci's challenge to the politics of the left in 'our times.' *International Journal of Lifelong Education, 14* (2), 120–143.

Allman, P., & Wallis, J. (1997). Commentary: Paulo Freire and the future of the radical tradition. *Studies in the Education of Adults, 29* (2), 113–120.

Amutabi, M., Jackson, K., Korsgaard, O., Murphy, P., Martin, T. Q., & Walters, S. (1997). Introduction. In S. Walters (Ed.), *Globalization, adult education and training: Impacts and issues* (pp. 1–12). London: Zed Books.

Anner, J. (1996). *Beyond identity politics: Emerging social justice movements in communities of color.* Boston: South End Press.

Apple, M. W. (1996). *Cultural politics and education.* New York: Teachers College Press.

Aptheker, H. (1967). *The nature of democracy, freedom, and revolution.* New York: International.

Armstrong, P. F. (1988). L'Ordine Nuovo: The legacy of Antonio Gramsci and the education of adults. *International Journal of Lifelong Education, 7* (4), 249–259.

Arvidson, L., & Stenøien, J. M. (1997). Knowledge and democracy: Old and new social movements as learning environments in the post-war welfare state. In P. Remes, S. Tøsse, P. Falkenerone, & B. Bergstedt (Eds.), *Social change and adult education research: Adult education in Nordic countries* (pp. 209–226). Jyväskylä, Finland: Institute of Educational Research, University of Jyväskylä.

Ayús, C. N., Cristóbal, A., Freyre, R. P., Gálvez, N., González, G. T., Monal, I., & Santana, J. L. (2000). Mesa redonda sobre sociedad civil [Roundtable on civil society]. *Revista Cubana de Ciencias Sociales, 31,* 3–36.

Beckman, B. (1993). The liberation of civil society: Neo-liberal theology and political theory. *Review of African Political Economy, 58,* 20–33.

Bellamy, R., & Schecter, D. (1993). *Gramsci and the Italian state.* Manchester, England: Manchester University Press.

Bergstedt, B. (1992). Postmodern learning process: The composition of knowledge in new social movements. In *Social change and adult education: Adult education research in Nordic countries, 1990/1991.* University of Norway. (ERIC Document Reproduction Service No. ED 351 510).

Berk, R. A. (1974). *Collective behavior.* Dubuque, IA: Brown.

Bernstein, E. (1911). Evolutionary socialism (E. C. Harvey, Trans.). New York: B. W. Huebsch.

Bloom, A., & Breines, W. (Eds.). (1995). *"Takin' it to the streets": A sixties reader.* New York: Oxford University Press.

Blumer, H. (1939). Collective behavior. In R. E. Park (Ed.), *An outline of the principles of sociology* (pp. 219–280). New York: Barnes & Noble.

Blumer, H. (1957). Collective behavior. In J. B. Gittler (Ed.), *Review of sociology: Analysis of a decade* (pp. 127–158). New York: Wiley.

Bobbio, N. (1979). Gramsci and the conception of civil society. In C. Mouffe (Ed.), *Gramsci and Marxist theory* (pp. 21–47). London: Routledge & Kegan Paul.

Boggs, C. (1976). *Gramsci's Marxism.* London: Pluto Press.

Boggs, C. (1983). The intellectuals and social movements: Some reflections on academic marxism. *Humanities and Society, 6* (2/3), 223–229.

Boggs, C. (1984). *The two revolutions: Gramsci and the dilemmas of Western Marxism.* Boston: South End Press.

Boggs, C. (1986). *Social movements and political power.* Philadelphia: Temple University Press.

Brass, T. (1991). Moral economists, subalterns, new social movements, and the (re-)emergence of a (post-)modernised (middle) peasant. *The Journal of Peasant Studies, 18,* 173–205.

Bron, A. (1995). Adult education and civil society in a comparative and historical perspective. In M. Bron, Jr., & M. Malewski (Eds.), *Adult education and democratic citizenship* (pp. 15–26). Wroclaw, Poland: Wroclaw University Press.

Brown, D. D. (1994). Discursive movements of identification. *Current Perspectives in Social Theory, 14,* 269–292.

Brown, R. W. (1954). Mass phenomena. In G. Lindsey (Ed.), *Handbook of social psychology: Vol. 2. Special fields and applications* (pp. 833–876). Reading, MA: Addison-Wesley.

Brown, T. (1999). Challenging globalization as discourse and phenomenon. *International Journal of Lifelong Learning, 18* (1), 3–17.

Brunt, R. (1989). The politics of identity. In S. Hall & M. Jacques (Eds.), *New times: The changing face of politics in the 1990s* (pp. 150–159). London: Lawrence & Wishart.

Buci-Glucksmann, C. (1980). *Gramsci and the state* (D. Fernbach, Trans.). London: Lawrence & Wishart.

Burawoy, M. (1989). Reflections on *Democracy and capitalism. Socialist Review, 19* (1), 59–74.

Burbach, R. (1998). The (un)defining of postmodern Marxism: On smashing modernization and narrating new social and economic actors. *Rethinking Marxism, 10* (1), 52–65.

Burbach, R., & Nuñez, O. (1987). *Fire in the Americas: Forging a revolutionary agenda.* London: Verso.

Burgess, J. S. (1944). The study of modern social movements as a means for clarifying the process of social action. *Social Forces, 22* (3), 271–275.

Calderón, F., & Santos, M. R. dos (1987). Movimientos sociales y gestación de cultura política. Pautas de interrogación [Social movements and gestation of political culture. Guidelines for questions]. In N. Lechner (Ed.), *Cultura política y democratización* (pp. 189–196). Santiago, Chile: CLACSO.

Cammett, J. M. (1967). *Antonio Gramsci and the origins of Italian communism.* Stanford, CA: Stanford University Press.

Cantril, H. (1941). *The psychology of social movements.* New York: Wiley.

Carroll, W. K., & Ratner, R. S. (1994). Between Leninism and radical pluralism: Gramscian reflections on counter-hegemony and the new social movements. *Critical Sociology, 20* (2), 3–26.

Cervero, R. M. (1991). Changing relationships between theory and practice. In J. M. Peters, P. Jarvis, & Associates. *Adult education: Evolution and achievements in a developing field of study* (pp. 19–41). San Francisco: Jossey-Bass.

Chandhoke, N. (1990). 'Bringing the people back in' political and intellectual agendas. *Economic and Political Weekly, 25,* 1721–1727.

Chase, A. (1977). *The legacy of Malthus: The social costs of the new scientific racism.* New York: Knopf.

Christensen, A. (1915). *Politics and crowd-morality* (A. C. Curtic, Trans.). New York: Dutton.

Clark, L. L. (1984). *Social Darwinism and France.* University of Alabama: University of Alabama Press.

Coben, D. (1995). Revisiting Gramsci. *Studies in the Education of Adults, 27* (1), 36–51.

Cohen, J. L. (1985). Strategy or identity: New theoretical paradigms and contemporary social movements. *Social Research, 52* (4), 663–716.

Cohen, J. L., & Arato, A. (1992). *Civil society and political theory.* Cambridge, MA: MIT Press.

Colletti, L. (1972). *From Rousseau to Lenin: Studies in ideology and society* (J. Merrington & J. White, Trans.). New York: Monthly Review Press.

Collins, M. (1991). *Adult education as vocation.* New York: Routledge.

Communist Labor Party. (1991). *Entering an epoch of social revolution.* Chicago: Author.

Conway, M. (1915). *The crowd in peace and war.* New York: Longmans, Green.

Cooper, L. (1998). From "Rolling Mass Action" to "RPL": The changing discourse of experience and learning in the South African labor movement. *Studies in Continuing Education, 20* (2), 143–157.

Crowther, J., & Shaw, M. (1997). Social movements and the education of desire. *Community Development Journal, 32* (3), 266–279.

Cunningham, P. M. (1988). The adult educator and social responsibility. In R. Brockett (Ed.), *Ethical issues in adult education* (pp. 133–145). New York: Teacher's Press.

Cunningham, P. M. (1996a, May). *Conceptualizing our work as adult educators in a socially responsible way.* Paper presented at the International Adult & Continuing Education Conference, Seoul, Korea. (ERIC Document Reproduction Service No. ED 401 410)

Cunningham, P. M. (1996b). Race, gender, class, and the practice of adult education in the United States. In P. Wangoola & F. Youngman (Eds.), *Towards a transformative political economy of adult education: Theoretical and practical challenges* (pp. 139–159). DeKalb, IL: LEPS Press.

Cunningham, P. M. (1998). The social dimension of transformative learning. *PAACE Journal of Lifelong Learning, 7,* 15–28.

D'Anieri, P., Ernst, C., & Kier, E. (1990). New social movements in historical perspective. *Comparative Politics, 22,* 445–458.

Darkenwald, G. G., & Merriam, S. B. (1982). *Adult education: Foundations of practice.* New York: Harper & Row.

David, M. L. (2000). Sociedad civil y participación en Cuba (part I) [Civil society and participation in Cuba]. *Revista Cubana de Ciencias Sociales, 31,* 37–70.

Davidson, A. (1977). *Antonio Gramsci.* London: Merlin.

Davis, J. (1930). *Contemporary social movements.* New York: Century.

Dobb, M. (1963). *Studies in the development of capitalism.* New York: International.

Dobbs, A. E. (1969). *Education and social movements, 1700–1850.* New York: Kelly. (Original work published 1919)

Dobson, A. (1989). *An introduction to the politics and philosophy of José Ortega y Gasset.* Cambridge: University of Cambridge Press.

Dykstra, C., & Law, M. (1994). Popular social movements as educative forces. In M. Hyams (Ed.), *Proceedings of the 35th Annual Adult Education Research Conference* (pp. 121–126). Knoxville: University of Tennessee.

Ehrenberg, J. (1992). *Dictatorship of the proletariat.* New York: Routledge.

Elsner, H., Jr. (1972). Introduction. In H. Elsner, Jr., (Ed.) & C. Elsner (Trans.),

The crowd and the public and other essays (pp. vii–xxv). Chicago: University of Chicago Press.

Engels, F. (1959). Ludwig Feuerbach and the end of classical German philosophy. In L. S. Feuer (Ed.), *Marx & Engels: Basic writings on politics and philosophy* (pp. 195–245). Garden City, NY: Anchor. (Original work published 1888)

Engels, F. (1978). *The origins of the family, private property and the state*. Peking: Foreign Languages Press. (Original work published 1891)

Engels, F. (1989). *Socialism: utopian and scientific* (E. Aveling, Trans.). New York: International. (Original work published 1880)

Entwistle, H. (1979). *Antonio Gramsci: Conservative schooling for radical politics*. London: Routledge & Kegan Paul.

Epstein, B. (1990). Rethinking social movement theory. *Socialist Review, 20* (1), 35–65.

Epstein, B. (1997). Postmodernism and the left. *New Politics, 6* (2), 130–144.

Escobar, A. (1992). Imagining a post-development era? Critical thought, development and social movements. *Social Text, 31/32,* 20–56.

Eyerman, R., & Jamison, A. (1991). *Social movements: A cognitive approach*. University Park, PA: Pennsylvania State University Press.

Faris, R. (1986). Building the social movement. In *Building the social movement* (pp. 5–11). Vancouver, British Columbia, Canada: University of British Columbia.

Federighi, P. (1997). Building the transnational dimension of adult education. *Convergence, 30* (2/3), 3–16.

Ferguson, A. (1966). *An essay on the history of civil society* (D. Forbes, Ed.). Edinburgh: University of Edinburgh. (Original work published 1767)

Ferree, M. M. (1992). The political context of rationality: Rational choice theory and resource mobilization. In A. D. Morris & C. M. Mueller (Eds.), *Frontiers in social movement theory*. New Haven, CT: Yale University Press.

Field, J. (1988). Workers' education and the crisis of British trade unionism. In T. Lovett (Ed.), *Radical approaches to adult education: A reader* (pp. 224–241). London: Routledge.

Field, J. (1995). Citizenship and identity: The significance for lifelong learning of Anthony Giddens' theory of "life politics." In M. Bron, Jr., & M. Malewski (Eds.), *Adult education and democratic citizenship* (pp. 31–46). Wroclaw, Poland: Wroclaw University Press.

Finger, M. (1989). New social movements and their implications for adult education. *Adult Education Quarterly, 40* (1), 15–22.

Finot, J. (1906). *Race prejudice* (F. Wade-Evans, Trans.). New York: Negro University Press.

Foley, G. (1993). Progressive but not socialist: Political education in the Zimbabwe liberation war. *Convergence, 26* (4), 8–18.

Foley, G. (1994). Adult education and capitalist reorganization. *Studies in the Education of Adults, 26* (2), 121–143.

Foley, G. (1999). *Learning in social action: A contribution to understanding informal education*. London: Zed Books.

Foner, P. S. (1947). *History of the labor movement in the United States* (Vol. 1). New York: International.

Foucault, M. (1980). *Power/knowledge: Selected interviews and other writings, 1972–*

1977 (C. Gordon, Ed., & C. Gordon, L. Marshall, J. Mepham, & K. Soper, Trans.). New York: Pantheon Books.

Foweraker, J. (1995). *Theorizing social movements*. Boulder, CO: Pluto Press.

Freire, P. (1978). *Pedagogy in process: The letters to Guinea-Bissau* (C. S. Hunter, Trans.). New York: Seabury Press.

Freire, P. (1984). *Pedagogy of the oppressed* (M. B. Ramos, Trans.). New York: Continuum.

Freire, P. (1993). *Pedagogy of the city* (D. Macedo, Trans.). New York: Continuum.

Fuentes, M., & Frank, A. G. (1989). Ten theses on social movements. *World Development, 17* (2), 179–191.

Fuentes, M., & Frank, A. G. (1990). Civil democracy: Social movements in recent world history. In S. Amin, G. Arrighi, A. G. Frank, & I. Wallerstein, *Transforming the revolution: Social movements and the world-system*. New York: Monthly Review Press.

Garner, R. (1997). Fifty years of social movement theory: An interpretation. In R. Garner & J. Tenuto, *Social movement theory and research: An annotated bibliographic guide* (pp. 1–58). Pasadena, CA: Scarecrow.

Gindin, S., & Panitch, L. (2000). Rekindling socialist imagination: Utopian vision and working-class capacities. *Monthly Review, 51* (10), 36–51.

Glick, C. E. (1948). Collective behavior in race relations. *American Sociological Review, 13* (3), 287–294.

Gorz, A. (1982). *Farewell to the working class: An essay on post-industrial socialism* (M. Sonenscher, Trans.). Boston: South End Press.

Gramsci, A. (1957). *The modern prince and other writings* (L. Marks, Trans.). New York: International.

Gramsci, A. (1971). *Selections from the prison notebooks* (Q. Hoare & G. N. Smith, Eds. & Trans.). New York: International.

Gramsci, A. (1994a). *Letters from prison, Vol. 2* (F. Rosengarten, Ed., & R. Rosenthal, Trans.). New York: Columbia University Press.

Gramsci, A. (1994b). *Pre-prison writings* (R. Bellamy, Ed., & V. Cox, Trans.) New York: Cambridge University Press.

Guéhenno, J. (1995). *The end of the nation-state* (V. Elliott, Trans.). Minneapolis, MN: University of Minnesota Press.

Guevara, E. C. (1994). *The Bolivian diary of Ernesto Che Guevara* (M. A. Waters, Ed.). New York: Pathfinder Press.

Habermas, J. (1970). *Toward a rational society: Student protest, science, and politics.* (J. J. Shapiro, Trans.). Boston: Beacon Press.

Habermas, J. (1981). New social movements. *Telos, 49*, 33–37.

Habermas, J. (1984). The tasks of a critical theory of society. In J. E. Bronner & D. M. Kellner (Eds.), *Critical theory and society: A reader* (pp. 292–312). New York: Routledge.

Habermas, J. (1989). *The structural transformation of the public sphere* (T. Burger, Trans.). Cambridge, MA: MIT Press.

Hall, B. (1978). Continuity in adult education and political struggle. *Convergence, 11* (1), 8–15.

Hall, B. (1988). Adult education and the peace movement. In T. Lovett (Ed.), *Radical approaches to adult education: A reader* (pp. 164–180). London: Routledge.

Hall, B. (1993). Learning and global civil society: Electronic networking in international non-governmental organizations. *International Journal of Canadian Adult Education and Training, 3* (3), 5–24.

Hall, B. (1996). Adult education and the political economy of global economic change. In P. Wangoola & F. Youngman (Eds.), *Towards a transformative political economy of adult education: Theoretical and practical challenges* (pp. 105–126). DeKalb, IL: LEPS Press.

Hall, B. (1997). *Adult learning, global civil society and politics.* Keynote presentation at the 16th annual Midwest Research-to-Practice in Adult, Continuing and Community Education conference, Michigan State University, East Lansing, Michigan.

Hayes, C.J.H. (1941). *A generation of materialism, 1871–1900.* New York: Harper & Brothers.

Haywood, H. (1978). *Black Bolshevik: Autobiography of an Afro-American communist.* Chicago: Liberator Press.

Heagerty, B., & Peery, N. (2000). *Moving onward: From racial division to class unity.* Chicago: People's Tribune/Tribuno del Pueblo.

Heaney, T. W. (1993). Identifying and dealing with vocational, social, and political issues. *New Directions for Adult and Continuing Education, 60,* 13–20.

Heberle, R. (1949). Observations on the sociology of social movements. *American Sociological Review, 14,* 346–357.

Heberle, R. (1968). Types and functions of social movements. In D. L. Sills (Ed.), *International encyclopedia of the social sciences* (Vol. 14, pp. 438–444). New York: Crowell & Collier and Macmillan.

Hegel, G.W.F. (1967). *Philosophy of right* (T. M. Knox, Trans.). New York: Oxford University. (Original work published 1821)

Holford, J. (1995). Why social movements matter: Adult education theory, cognitive praxis, and the creation of knowledge. *Adult Education Quarterly, 45* (2), 95–111.

Holst, J. D. (1999). The affinities of Lenin and Gramsci: Implications for radical adult education theory and practice. *International Journal of Lifelong Education, 18* (5), 407–421.

Horton, M., & Freire, P. (1990). *We make the road by walking: Conversations on education and social change* (B. Bell, J. Gaventa, & J. Peters, Eds.). Philadelphia: Temple University Press.

Howlett, D. (1991). Social movement and development education. *Canadian and International Education, 20* (1), 125–130.

Ibarruri, D. (1966). *They shall not pass: The autobiography of La Pasionaria* (D. Ibarruri, Trans.). New York: International.

Jackson, K. (1995). Popular education and the state: A new look at the community debate. In M. Mayo & J. Thompson (Eds.), *Adult learning, critical intelligence and social change* (pp. 182–203). Leicester, England: NIACE.

Jarvis, P. (1993). *Adult education and the state.* New York: Routledge.

Jenkins, J. C. (1995). Social movements, political representation, and the state: An agenda and comparative framework. In J. C. Jenkins & B. Klandermans (Eds.), *The politics of social protest: Comparative perspectives on states and social movements* (pp. 14–35). Minneapolis, MN: University of Minnesota Press.

Kastner, A. (1990, June). *Popular movements and adult education.* Paper presented at the 9th Annual Conference of the Canadian Association for the Study of Adult Education, Victoria, British Columbia.

Katz, D. (1940). The psychology of the crowd. In J. P. Guilford (Ed.), *Fields of psychology* (pp. 145–162). New York: Van Nostrand.

Keane, J. (1988). *Democracy and civil society*. London: Verso.

Keane, J. (1998). *Civil society: Old images, new visions*. Stanford, CA: Stanford University Press.

Keller, J. F. (1983). *Power in America: The southern question and the control of labor*. Chicago: Vanguard Books.

Kilgore, D. W. (1999). Understanding learning in social movements: A theory of collective learning. *International Journal of Lifelong Learning, 18* (3), 191–202.

Kincheloe, J. L., Steinberg, S., & McLaren, P. (1998). Series editors' preface. In J. L. Kincheloe, S. Steinberg, & P. McLaren (Eds.), *Power/knowledge/pedagogy: The meaning of democratic education in unsettling times* (pp. vii–ix). Boulder, CO: Westview Press.

Kivisto, P. (1986). What's new about the "new social movements"?: Continuities and discontinuities with the socialist project. *Mid-American Review of Sociology, 11* (2), 29–44.

Klandermans, B. (1991). New social movements and resource mobilization: The European and the American approach revisited. In D. Rucht (Ed.), *Research in social movements*. Boulder, CO: Westview Press.

Klandermans, B. (1997). *The social psychology of protest*. Cambridge, MA: Blackwell.

Knowles, M. S. (1977). *A history of the adult education movement in the United States*. New York: Krieger.

Korsgaard, O. (1997). The impact of globalization on adult education. In S. Walters (Ed.), *Globalization, adult education and training: Impacts and issues* (pp. 15–26). London: Zed Books.

Kothari, R. (1993). The yawning vacuum: A world without alternatives. *Alternatives, 18*, 119–139.

Kuhn, T. S. (1970). *The structure of scientific revolutions* (2nd ed.). Chicago: University of Chicago Press.

Laclau, E., & Mouffe, C. (1985). *Hegemony and socialist strategy: Towards a radical democratic politics*. London: Verso.

Laclau, E., & Mouffe, C. (1987). Post-Marxism without apologies. *New Left Review, 166*, 79–106.

LaPiere, R. T. (1938). *Collective behavior*. New York: McGraw-Hill.

League of Revolutionaries for a New America (1998, October). Building a movement: What's the LRNA strategy? *People's Tribune/Tribuno del Pueblo*, p. 2.

LeBon, G. (1974). *The psychology of peoples*. New York: Arno Press. (Original work published in 1894)

LeBon, G. (1896). *The crowd: A study of the popular mind*. London: Benn.

Lenin, V. I. (1939). *Imperialism: The highest stage of capitalism*. New York: International. (Originally published in 1917)

Lenin, V. I. (1943). *State and revolution*. New York: International.

Lenin, V. I. (1969). *On proletarian culture*. Moscow: Novosti Press Agency. (Original work published 1920)

Lenin, V. I. (1970). *What is to be done?* (2nd ed.). Peking: Foreign Languages Press. (Original work published in 1902)

Lindeman, E. C. (1921). *The community: An introduction to the study of community leadership and organization.* New York: Association Press.

Lindeman, E. C. (1961). *The meaning of adult education.* Norman, OK: Oklahoma Research Center for Continuing Professional and Higher Education. (Original work published 1926)

Linds, W. (1991). Walking together: Development education and Canada's social movements. *Canadian and International Education, 20* (1), 131–142.

Locke, J. (1952). Concerning the true original extent of civil government. In R. M. Hutchins (Ed.), *Great books of the western world: Vol. 35. Locke, Berkeley, Hume* (pp. 25–81). Chicago: Encyclopædia Britannica. (Original work published 1690)

Lovett, T. (1988a). Conclusion: Radical adult education. In T. Lovett (Ed.), *Radical approaches to adult education: A reader* (pp. 300–302). London: Routledge.

Lovett, T. (1988b). Introduction. In T. Lovett (Ed.), *Radical approaches to adult education: A reader* (pp. xv–xxiii). London: Routledge.

Lovett, T. (Ed.). (1988c). *Radical approaches to adult education: A reader.* London: Routledge.

Lovett, T., Clarke, C., & Kilmurray, A. (Eds.). (1983). *Adult education and community action.* London: Croom Helm.

Luke, T. W. (1994). Ecological politics and local struggles: Earth First! as an environmental resistance movement. *Current Perspectives in Social Theory, 14,* 241–267.

Luxemburg, R. (1970a). Reform or revolution. In M. A. Waters (Ed.), *Rosa Luxemburg speaks* (pp. 51–128). New York: Pathfinder Press. (Original work published 1900)

Luxemburg, R. (1970b). The Junius pamphlet: The crisis in the social democracy. In M. A. Waters (Ed.), *Rosa Luxemburg speaks* (pp. 353–453). New York: Pathfinder Press. (Original work published 1916)

Magdoff, H. (1998). A letter to a contributor: The same old state. *Monthly Review, 49* (8), 1–10.

Maier, N.R.F. (1942). The role of frustration in social movements. *The Psychological Review, 49* (6), 586–599.

Mandel, E. (1975). *Late capitalism* (J. De Bres, Trans.). London: Verso.

Manicom, L., & Walters, S. (1997). Feminist popular education in the light of globalization. In S. Walters (Ed.), *Globalization, adult education and training: Impacts and issues* (pp. 69–78). London: Zed Books.

Martin, B. (1988). Education and the environmental movement. In T. Lovett (Ed.), *Radical approaches to adult education: A reader* (pp. 202–223). London: Routledge.

Martin, E. D. (1923). Some mechanisms which distinguish the crowd from other forms of behavior. *Journal of Abnormal Psychology and Social Psychology, 18* (3), 187–203.

Martin, T. Q. (1997). Women, poverty and adult education in Chile. In S. Walters (Ed.), *Globalization, adult education and training: Impacts and issues* (pp. 39–46). London: Zed Books.

Marx, K. (1959). *Economic and philosophic manuscripts of 1844* (M. Milligan, Trans.). Moscow: Progress.

Marx, K. (1974). The eighteenth Brumaire of Louis Bonaparte. In D. Fernbach (Ed.), *Surveys from exile* (pp. 146–249). New York: Vintage.

Marx, K. (1975). On the Jewish question. In K. Marx & F. Engels, *Collected works* (Vol. 3, pp. 146–174). New York: International. (Original work published 1844)

Marx, K. (1977a). *Capital, Vol. 1* (B. Fowkes, Trans.). New York: Vintage Books. (Original work published 1867)

Marx, K. (1977b). *Selected writings* (D. McLellan, Ed.). New York: Oxford University Press.

Marx, K., & Engels, F. (1948). *The communist manifesto.* New York: International. (Originally published in 1848)

Marx, K., & Engels, F. (1959). *Basic writings on politics and philosophy* (L. S. Feuer, Ed.). Garden City, NJ: Anchor Books.

Marx, K., & Engels, F. (1976). *The German ideology.* Moscow: Progress.

Marx, K., & Engels, F. (1978). *The Marx-Engels reader* (2nd ed.) (R. C. Tucker, Ed.). New York: Norton.

Mayo, M., & Thompson, J. (Eds.). (1995). *Adult learning, critical intelligence and social change.* London: NIACE.

Mayo, P. (1993). When does it work? Freire's pedagogy in context. *Studies in the Education of Adults, 25* (1), 11–30.

Mayo, P. (1994a). Gramsci, Freire, and radical adult education: A few "blind spots." *Humanity & Society, 18* (3), 82–98.

Mayo, P. (1994b). Synthesizing Gramsci and Freire: Possibilities for a theory of radical adult education. *International Journal of Lifelong Education, 13* (2), 125–148.

McCormick, T. J. (1967). *China market: America's quest for informal empire, 1893–1901.* Chicago: Quadrangle Books.

McDougall, W. (1920). *The group mind.* New York: Putnam.

McDougall, W. (1961). William McDougall. In C. Murchison (Ed.), *A history of psychology in autobiography* (Vol. 1, pp. 191–231). New York: Russell & Russell.

McDougall, W. (1977). *Is America safe for democracy?* New York: Arno Press. (Original work published 1921)

McIlroy, J. (1995). The dying of the light? A radical look at trade union education. In M. Mayo & J. Thompson (Eds.), *Adult learning, critical intelligence and social change* (pp. 146–168). Leicester, England: NIACE.

McLaren, P. (2000). *Che Guevara, Paulo Freire, and the pedagogy of revolution.* Lanham, MD: Rowman & Littlefield.

McNally, D. (1997). Language, history and class struggle. In E. M. Wood & J. B. Foster (Eds.), *In defense of history: Marxism and the postmodern agenda* (pp. 26–42). New York: Monthly Review Press.

Meadows, P. (1943). Movements of social withdrawal. *Sociology and Social Research, 29,* 46–50.

Melucci, A. (1981). Ten hypotheses for the analysis of new movements. In Diana Pinto (Ed.), *Contemporary Italian sociology* (pp. 173–194). Cambridge, England: Cambridge University Press.

Melucci, A. (1984). An end to social movements? *Social Science Information, 23,* 819–835.

Melucci, A. (1989). *Nomads of the present: Social movements and individual needs in contemporary society* (J. Keane & P. Mier, Eds.). Philadelphia: Temple University Press.

Melucci, A. (1992). Liberation or meaning? Social movements, culture and democracy. *Development and Change, 23* (3), 43–77.

Mills, C. W. (1962). *The Marxists.* New York: Dell.

Milton, D. (1982). *The politics of U.S. labor: From the Great Depression to the New Deal.* New York: Monthly Review Press.

Moody, K. (1997). *Workers in a lean world: Unions in the international economy.* London: Verso.

Morgan, W. J. (1987). The pedagogical politics of Antonio Gramsci—"pessimism of the intellect, optimism of the will." *International Journal of Lifelong Education, 6* (4), 295–308.

Moscovici, S. (1985). *The age of the crowd* (J. C. Whitehouse, Trans.). New York: Cambridge University Press.

Mueller, C. M. (1992). Building social movement theory. In A. D. Morris & C. M. Mueller (Eds.), *Frontiers in social movement theory.* New Haven, CT: Yale University Press.

Mukasa, H. (1996). The nature of imperialism in the 1990s and the implications for adult education. In P. Wangoola & F. Youngman (Eds.), *Towards a transformative political economy of adult education: Theoretical and practical challenges* (pp. 89–104). DeKalb, IL: LEPS Press.

Murphy, M. (2000). Adult education, lifelong learning and the end of political economy. *Studies in the Education of Adults, 32* (2), 166–180.

Naiman, J. (1996). Left feminism and the return to class. *Monthly Review, 48* (2), 12–28.

Navarro, V. (1988). Social movements and class politics in the US. In R. Miliband, L. Panitch, & J. Saville (Eds.), *The socialist register, 1988* (pp. 425–447). London: Merlin Press.

Navarro, V. (1991). The limitations of legitimation and Fordism and the possibility for socialist reforms. *Rethinking Marxism, 4* (2), 27–60.

Neidhardt, F., & Rucht, D. (1991). The analysis of social movements: The state of the art and some perspectives for further research. In D. Rucht (Ed.), *Research on social movements.* Boulder, CO: Westview Press.

Nugent, D. (1997). Northern intellectuals and EZLN. In E. M. Wood & J. B. Foster (Eds.), *In defense of history: Marxism and the postmodern agenda* (pp. 163–174). New York: Monthly Review Press.

Núñez Soto, O. (1989). Social movements in the struggle for democracy, revolution, and socialism. *Rethinking Marxism, 2* (1), 7–22.

Nzimande, B., & Sikhosana, M. (1995a). "Civil society," mass organizations and the national liberation movement in South Africa. In L. M. Sachikonye (Ed.), *Democracy, civil society and the state* (pp. 47–65). Harare, Zimbabwe: SAPES.

Nzimande, B., & Sikhosana, M. (1995b). "Civil society": A theoretical survey and critique of some South African conceptions. In L. M. Sachikonye (Ed.), *Democracy, civil society and the state* (pp. 20–45). Harare, Zimbabwe: SAPES.

Obadele, I. A. (1972, February). The struggle is for land. *Black Scholar*, 24–32.

O'Cadiz, M. & Torres, C. A. (1994). Literacy, social movements, and class consciousness: Paths from Freire and the São Paulo experience. *Anthropology Education Quarterly, 25* (3), 208–225.

Ortega y Gasset, J. (1960). *The revolt of the masses.* New York: Norton. (Original work published 1932)

Osorio, J. (1995). Adult education in Latin America from the focus of a critical modernity. *International Journal of University Adult Education, 34* (3), 53–56.

Osorio, J. (1997). Rethinking popular education: An interim balance. *Adult Education and Development, 48,* 9–17.

Palma, D. (1991). *La democracia en Latinoamérica* [Democracy in Latin America]. Santiago, Chile: CEAAL.

Park, R. E. (1939). Symbiosis and socialization: A frame reference for the study of society. *American Journal of Sociology, 45,* 1–25.

Park, R. E. (1972). *The crowd and the public and other essays* (H. Elsner, Jr., Ed., & C. Elsner, Trans.). Chicago: University of Chicago Press. (Original work published 1904)

Paulston, R. G., & Altenbaugh, R. J. (1988). Adult education in radical U.S. social and ethnic movements: From case studies to typology to explanation. In T. Lovett (Ed.), *Radical approaches to adult education: A reader* (pp. 114–137). London: Routledge.

Peery, N. (1978). *The Negro national colonial question* (2nd ed.). Chicago: Workers Press.

Phelps, C. (1995). Lenin, Gramsci and Marzani. *Monthly Review, 47* (6), 53–54.

Philion, S. (1998). Bridging the gap between new social movement theory and class. *Rethinking Marxism, 10* (4), 79–104.

Picón, C. (1996). State and civil society in the perspective of adult education in Latin America. In P. Wangoola & F. Youngman (Eds.), *Towards a transformative political economy of adult education: Theoretical and practical challenges* (pp. 75–86). DeKalb, IL: LEPS Press.

Piven, F. F. (1995). Globalizing capitalism and the rise of identity politics. In L. Panitch (Ed.), *Socialist review 1995* (pp. 102–116). London: Merlin Press.

Plotke, D. (1990). What's so new about new social movements? *Socialist register, 20* (1), 81–111.

Reed, D. (1981). *Education for building a people's movement.* Boston: South End Press.

Rehmann, J. (1999). "Abolition" of civil society?: Remarks on a widespread misunderstanding in the interpretations of "civil society." *Socialism and Democracy, 13* (2), 1–18.

Robeson, P. (1958). *Here I stand.* Boston: Beacon Press.

Ross, E. A. (1916). *Social psychology.* New York: Macmillan.

Ross, G. (1995). Saying no to capitalism at the millennium. In L. Panitch (Ed.), *Socialist register, 1995* (pp. 50–74). London: Merlin Press.

Rubenson, K. (1989). The sociology of adult education. In S. M. Merriam & P. M. Cunningham (Eds.), *The handbook of adult and continuing education* (pp. 51–69). San Francisco: Jossey-Bass.

Sachikonye, L. M. (1995). Democracy, civil society and social movements: An analytical framework. In L. M. Sachikonye (Ed.), *Democracy, civil society and the state* (pp. 1–19). Harare, Zimbabwe: SAPES.

Sassoon, A. S. (1987). *Gramsci's politics* (2nd ed.). Minneapolis, MN: University of Minnesota Press.

Sayers, S. (1980). On the Marxist dialectic. In S. Sayers & R. Norman, *Hegel, Marx, and dialectic: A debate* (pp. 1–24). Atlantic Highlands, NJ: Humanities Press.

Schied, F. M. (1993). *Learning in social context.* DeKalb, IL: LEPS Press.

Schuurman, F. J. (1993). Modernity, post-modernity and the new social movements. In F. J. Schuurman (Ed.), *Beyond the impasse: New directions in development theory* (pp. 187–206). London: Zed Books.

Segal, L. (1991). Whose left? Socialism, feminism and the future. *New Left Review,* 185, 81–91.

Seligman, A. B. (1992). *The idea of civil society.* New York: Free Press.

Selman, G. (1990, June). *New social movements and citizenship education in Canada.* Paper presented at the 9th Annual Conference of the Canadian Association for the Study of Adult Education, Victoria, British Columbia.

Shor, I., & Freire, P. (1987). *A pedagogy of liberation.* Westport, CT: Bergin & Garvey.

Shukra, K. (1997). The death of a black political movement. *Community Development Journal,* 32 (3), 233–243.

Slater, D. (1991). New social movements and old political questions. *International Journal of Political Economy,* 21 (1), 32–65.

Slater, D. (1994). Power and social movements in the other occident: Latin America in an international context. *Latin American Perspectives,* 21 (2), 11–37.

Smelser, N. (1962). *Theory of collective behavior.* New York: Free Press.

Sociedad civil en debate [Civil society in debate]. [Special issue]. (1999). *Temas,* 16–17.

Spencer, B. (1995). Old and new social movements as learning sites: Greening labor unions and unionizing the greens. *Adult Education Quarterly,* 46 (1), 31–42.

Stein, L. von. (1964). *The history of the social movement in France, 1789–1850* (K. Mengleberg, Ed. & Trans.). Totowa, NJ: Bedminster. (Original work published 1850)

Strauss, A. L. (1944). The literature on panic. *Journal of Abnormal and Social Psychology,* 39, 317–328.

Strauss, A. L. (1947). Research in collective behavior: Neglect and need. *American Sociological Review,* 12, 352–354.

Stubblefield, H. W. (1988). *Towards a history of adult education in America.* London: Croom Helm.

Swart, K. W. (1964). *The sense of decadence in nineteenth-century France.* The Hague, Netherlands: Martinus Nijhoff.

Sweezy, P. M. (1942). *The theory of capitalist development.* New York: Monthly Review Press.

Sweezy, P. M. (1997). More (or less) on globalization. *Monthly Review,* 49 (4), 1–4.

Tabb, W. K. (1997). Globalization is an issue, the power of capital is the issue. *Monthly Review,* 49 (2), 20–30.

Taylor, V. (1997). The trajectory of national liberation and social movements: The South African experience. *Community Development Journal, 32,* 252–265.

Texier, J. (1979). Gramsci, theoretician of the superstructures. In C. Mouffe (Ed.), *Gramsci and Marxist theory* (pp. 48–79). London: Routledge & Kegan Paul.

Thompson, J. L. (Ed.). (1980a). *Adult education for a change.* London: Hutchinson.

Thompson, J. L. (1980b). Adult education for a change. In J. L. Thompson (Ed.), *Adult education for a change* (pp. 219–223). London: Hutchinson.

Thompson, J. L. (1983). *Learning liberation: Women's responses to men's education.* London: Croom Helm.

Thompson, J. L. (1993). Learning, liberation and maturity: An open letter to who-ever's left. *Adults Learning, 4* (9), 244.

Torres, C. A. (1990). *The politics of nonformal education in Latin America.* New York: Praeger.

Torres, C. A. (1994). Paulo Freire as secretary of education in the municipality of São Paulo. *Comparative Education Review, 30* (2), 181–214.

Touraine, A. (1985). An introduction to the study of social movements. *Social Research, 52* (4), 749–787.

Trotter, W. (1919). *Instincts of the herd in peace and war.* New York: Macmillan.

Tucker, K. H. (1991). How new are new social movements? *Theory, Culture & Society, 8* (2), 75–98.

Turner, R. H., & Killian, L. M. (1957). *Collective behavior.* Englewood Cliffs, NJ: Prentice-Hall.

Umar, A. (1993). The protest tradition in Nigerian adult education: An analysis of NEPU's emancipatory learning project, 1950–1966. *Convergence, 26* (4), 19–32.

Wainwright, H. (1995). Once more moving on: Social movements, political representation and the future of the radical left. In L. Panitch (Ed.), *Socialist register, 1995* (pp. 75–101). London: Merlin Press.

Weatherford, J. (1988). *Indian givers.* New York: Fawcett Columbine.

Welton, M. (1993). Social revolutionary learning: The new social movements as learning sites. *Adult Education Quarterly, 43* (3), 152–164.

Welton, M. (1995a). In defense of the lifeworld: A Habermasian approach to adult learning. In M. Welton (Ed.), *In defense of the lifeworld: Critical perspectives on adult learning* (pp. 127–156). Albany, NY: State University of New York Press.

Welton, M. (1995b). Introduction. In M. Welton (Ed.), *In defense of the lifeworld: Critical perspectives on adult learning* (pp. 1–10). Albany, NY: State University of New York Press.

Welton, M. (1997). In defense of civil society: Canadian adult education in neo-conservative times. In S. Walters (Ed.), *Globalization, adult education and training: Impacts and issues* (pp. 27–38). London: Zed Books.

Wilde, L. (1990). Class analysis and the politics of new social movements. *Capital and Class, 42,* 52–78.

Wirth, L. (1940). Ideological aspects of social disorganization. *American Sociological Review, 5* (4), 472–482.

Wolpe, H. (1970). Some problems concerning revolutionary consciousness. In R. Miliband & J. Saville (Eds.), *The socialist register* (pp. 251–280). London: Merlin Press.

Wood, E. M. (1994, June 13). Identity crisis. *In These Times, 18*, 28–29.

Wood, E. M. (1997). Labor, the state, and class struggle. *Monthly Review, 49* (3), 1–17.

Wood, E. M. (1998a). Class compacts, the welfare state, and epochal shifts. *Monthly Review, 49* (8), 24–43.

Wood, E. M. (1998b). *The communist manifesto* after 150 years. *Monthly Review, 50* (1), 14–35.

Wood, E. M. (1998c). *The retreat from class: A new "true" socialism* (Rev. ed.). London: Verso.

Workers' Educational Association [WEA]. (1998). *Workers' education, civil society and international development*. London: Author.

Wright, E. O. (1979). *Class, crisis, and the state*. London: Verso.

Wright, E. O. (1985). *Classes*. London: Verso.

Yarnit, M. (1980). Second Chance to Learn, Liverpool: Class and adult education. In J. L. Thompson (Ed.), *Adult education for a change* (pp. 174–191). London: Hutchinson.

Yarnit, M. (1995). Piecing together the fragments: Thoughts on adult education in a vanished era. In M. Mayo & J. Thompson (Eds.), *Adult learning, critical intelligence and social change* (pp. 69–81). Leicester, England: NIACE.

Youngman, F. (1986). *Adult education and socialist pedagogy*. London: Croom Helm.

Youngman, F. (1996a). A transformative political economy of adult education: An introduction. In P. Wangoola & F. Youngman (Eds.), *Towards a transformative political economy of adult education: Theoretical and practical challenges* (pp. 3–30). DeKalb, IL: LEPS Press.

Youngman, F. (1996b). Towards a political economy of adult education and development in Botswana. In P. Wangoola & F. Youngman (Eds.), *Towards a transformative political economy of adult education: Theoretical and practical challenges* (pp. 191–222). DeKalb, IL: LEPS Press.

Youngman, F. (2000). *The political economy of adult education and development*. London: Zed Books.

Zacharakis-Jutz, J. (1991, April). *Highlander Folkschool and the labor movement, 1932–1953*. Paper presented at the American Educational Research Association, Chicago, Illinois. (ERIC Document Reproduction Service No. ED 331 940)

Zald, M. N. (1992). Looking backward to look forward: Reflections on the past and future of the resource mobilization research program. In A. D. Morris & C. M. Mueller (Eds.), *Frontiers in social movement theory*. New Haven: Yale University Press.

Index

Abernathy, Ralph, 84–85

Activism, Freire on, 79

Adam, Barry, 45, 46

Adult education: ability to change society, 78–80, 96; choice of philosophy, 2, 89; civil societarian as neo-liberal, 74–75; importance of political economy for, 87, 91–92; informal, 80; Lenin and, 80; neo-liberalism and NGOs, 101–2; political nature of, 77, 80; problem of psychology and, 86; professionalization of, 5, 81; radical, 2; radical, civil society and social movements, 3–4, 7, 74–75, 77–78, 96–102; radical, defined, 4–5; radical, Gramsci, 7, 103, 106, 108–11, 112–13; radical, hegemony and, 89, 90–93, 106–15; radical, history of, 5, 77; radical, informal nature of in social movements, 91; radical, marginalization of, 5, 78; radical, nature of, 78–79; radical, old social movements as important sites for, 93–94; radical, political party, 108–15; radical, politics of social movements and, 6–7, 17, 93–97, 99–102, 112–13; radical, radical pluralist perspectives, 81–87; radical, in social movements, 5, 79, 80–93; radical, social relations in, 91; radical, socialist perspectives on, 87–93; radical, theory and, 4, 101–2, 114–15; social movements as revitalization of roots of, 78; tendency to dismiss learning in social movements, 80–81

Albert, Michael, 103

Alexander, David, 93, 94, 97, 99

Alforja-Cepis, 96

Alienation, 11–12, 64, 90. *See also* Dialectics; Historical materialism; Marxism

Alliances, 41–43, 93–95; Gramsci and, 111–12

Allman, Paula, 88–93, 94, 95, 102, 104, 113

Altenbaugh, Richard, 78

Amin, Samir, 2

Amutabi, Maurice, 97

Anner, John, 51

Anti-racism movement, 47, 93, 94. *See also* Black Power; Civil Rights movement

Aptheker, Herber, 73

About the Author

JOHN D. HOLST is Assistant Professor, Department of Curriculum & Instruction, University of St. Thomas, Minneapolis.